Communication In Relationships

How To Build And Maintain
Bonds With People In Life, Love,
And The Workplace

SHIRLEY COLE

Legal & Disclaimer

The following document is reproduced below with the goal of providing information that is as accurate and reliable as possible.

This declaration is deemed fair and valid by both the American Bar Association and the Committee of Publishers Association and is legally binding throughout the United States.

Furthermore, the transmission, duplication or reproduction of any of the following work including specific information will be considered an illegal act irrespective of if it is done electronically or in print. This extends to creating

way be considered an endorsement from the trademark holder.

Table of Contents

Introduction

There are few things more difficult and frustrating than relationships. Romantic or otherwise, navigating the interpersonal bonds that make up our social networks can be a stressful and confusing process. Romantic relationships, though, are especially trying. When two people are committed to being together, they have to work through issues that might on some level make them want to just give up. What many people fail to realize is just how much hard work is really required to make a relationship successful and to allow both halves of the whole to flourish, both together and individually; to achieve all of their dreams both independently and as a team. When two people are in a committed long-term relationship, there is a sort of symbiosis that occurs. While both individuals are distinctly separate, they also come together and create something new and unique, something far greater than the sum of its parts. Think of a long term relationship between two people like a project they are co-creators of. They form an incredibly intimate bond together and get to know each other to such a deep and thorough extent that no one else knows either of them better than they know each other. The reason why a relationship is such a complex and confusing enterprise is a direct result of this bond. Whatever happens to one partner deeply affects the other, whether they want it to or not. Everything that happens to each of them becomes the direct business and problem of the other. In order for both parties to be happy and fulfilled under these circumstances, a great deal of communication and teamwork is required.

Both of these skills are difficult to practice even at the best of times when everything is smooth and rosy and the relationship is ticking over nicely. When times get hard, however, our ability to put these skills into practice is really put to the test. There's a good reason why between forty and fifty percent of marriages end in divorce. Nothing lasts in this world and making a relationship really go the distance is an incredibly hard thing to do. A lifetime is a long time, and it's a very long time to put up with all the inevitably annoying and troubling aspects of our partner's character, no matter how much we love them. Relationships don't usually break down due to a lack of love. If love was all that was needed to make things work, the divorce rate would be much lower than it is. Relationships can fall apart for any number of reasons, but the causes almost always stem from the same root problem: a lack of good communication.

Every relationship faces problems, and every couple will be tested. A good, strong relationship isn't about being perfect or keeping a squeaky clean record. It's about rising to every challenge and overcoming all the obstacles you face. It's about being able to admit when you're wrong and making a genuine effort to try to make things better. It's about not giving up, no matter what, and having each other's backs until the end. A strong relationship is one based on teamwork, not competition. It's one that approaches problems with a mentality of 'how do we handle this together?' and then looking for solutions, rather than blaming each other and dwelling on the problems themselves. It's not you versus them, it's the two of you versus the issue, every time.

Many couples find it very difficult to properly communicate with each other. They struggle to find the right words to say or the right state of mind to properly connect at the same time. This lack of communication leads to arguments and fights which only make the problem worse, allowing emotions to spiral out of control and feelings to get hurt. It's common for two people who love each other more than anything to lay awake at night crying, one in their bed and the other on the couch, each wishing their partner could see things the way they do. Many relationships are characterized not by mutual support but by petty fights and bickering that

SHIRLEY COLE

never seem to end. Couples fail to listen to each other or approach problem's together, instead preferring to focus on who's to blame or who's done something to hurt the other. Instead of showing love and affection to one another, there is more often than not an atmosphere of tension and resentment. All of these issues ultimately boil down to a lack of effective, calm, empathetic, loving communication.

When a relationship is based around a mutual bond of trust and openness that facilitates this type of vitally important communication, it's much harder for problems to take root and grow in the same way that they do in relationships that lack it. The majority of issues that arise throughout the course of a relationship can be worked out just through sitting down and calmly discussing them from both people's points of view, no matter how long it might take or how many times you might have to say something to get your point across. Communication is a skill, and like any skill, it takes a lot of practice to get good at it. No matter the difficulties that you and your partner face, you can both learn how to communicate in a way that allows you to overcome them. Whether you feel like you're not being heard, or your partner thinks that you don't understand them, or you just want to be able to have a conversation about your problems without it descending into fighting or yelling, this book contains the information you need to break new ground and move your relationship with each other to the next level.

This book will provide you with the tools you need to begin communicating well and improve your relationships in every aspect of your life. Although it focuses primarily on relationships of the romantic kind, it also discusses navigating more platonic relationships at length, and many of the lessons that can be learned from romantic relationships can be applied elsewhere in your life. I wrote this book by drawing from the lessons I've learned from years of studying relationships and helping couples to cooperate.

Over the course of my career as a professional family therapist, since I started back in 2004, I've coached hundreds of people on moving through difficulties they faced in their lives and relationships. I love to help people, and being able to assist others in getting through the tough situations we all face is an incredibly fulfilling experience for me. It was this passion and drive that inspired to collect my thoughts and lessons into this book as a way to spread the knowledge I have to as wide an audience as possible. It will deliver simple, practical, proven techniques for improving relationships — that's any relationship with anyone in your life, not just with your partner. With the advice this book contains, you'll learn how to think, talk, and act in order to repair holes in your relationships and resolve or prevent arguments so that you can provide your loved ones with the support they deserve. The things we'll be talking about over the course of the next few chapters will revolutionize the way you treat the people that you care about most in life, ensuring it's your one-stop-guide to improving your relationships, maintaining a loving, lasting bond with your partner, and preventing issues from tearing you apart from the things that matter the most to you.

Couples who can communicate effectively are more likely to have a happy, fulfilling, lasting relationship than those who can't. Communicating well allows you to pick up on when something is wrong so that you can nip it in the bud by addressing it before it has the chance to grow into a larger and further reaching problem. When you can sit down and properly talk about the issues you face with your partner, with the freedom for each of you to be heard and allowed the time and space to properly make your case, you can sort problems out before they have a chance to fester and cause deep resentment and emotional scars. My clients, old and new, tell me on a regular basis that the things I've taught them have helped them to change their lives and put themselves and their relationships on the right path. If you were to go to couples therapy with me, I'd be telling you the exact same things that I outline in this book; overcoming the obstacles that any relationship faces about being able to give each other the chance to express how you feel about every aspect of the problems you face. It's only when we adopt this attitude of openness, patience, and understanding that we feel like we can be heard, enlightened as to how our partner feels, and able to put problems in the past while learning from our mistakes and going forward together.

No matter how much you might love your partner, you can't read their mind. You need to give them the opportunity to tell you how they really feel, and you need to be able to accept whatever they say, regardless of your own private feelings about it. Their feelings matter, and if you can't or won't validate the way they feel they'll only grow to resent you in the long run. This book is a promise; it's a promise to you that you have what it takes to fix your relationship. With the help of this book, you *will* see a tangible difference in the way you and your partner work together. You *will* learn how to make your relationship happy, lasting, and loving, and you *will* become wiser, more emotionally intelligent person. Without learning the lessons that this book contains, how might your relationship play out in the long run? How long do you think you can make things last if you don't fully understand and appreciate the basic building blocks necessary to actually get into the trenches and do the heavy lifting? Will you be able to come to solutions on problems and move on for good without half-solved issues coming back to haunt you in the future? Every second you delay is a second of the time you have with your partner that ticks away, frustrated and confused when it could and should be calm and loving. Don't wait. Change your relationship now! Change your life, change your happiness, and gain the skills you need to in order to make your relationship last and create a lifetime of happy and fulfilling memories that you can share with the people closest to you.

Chapter One: Positive Communication

In this chapter, you'll learn how to communicate in a positive and productive manner. Before we can go into the best ways to communicate, it's important to understand the gulf in processing and understanding communication that exists between men and women.

Differences in Male and Female Communication

Communication is a highly relative concept. All of us communicate slightly differently, in our own individual ways, much like everybody's fingerprints seem similar at a glance, but each person is unique. In addition to this, we can also identify differing trends in how men and women communicate. Men tend to rely more on logic and reasoning in order to communicate and relate. They see things more mechanically, with an emphasis on problem-solving and wanting to fix things. When they encounter a situation they need to overcome, men are more likely to want to break it down and work out how to solve any problems in order to address the issue as it is and then move on. Women, however, tend to be more emotionally focused. They are more likely to use relational examples in order to communicate their thoughts and rely on talking about their problems in order to work out how they feel and then work through and fix their problems on their own and in their own time, rather than forcing a solution straight away. Women, therefore, feel a desire to be heard and validated by their partners, whereas men often feel discussing the emotional side of things is unnecessary as long as they solve the root problem.

This difference in communication can lead to a great deal of difficulty when problems arise in relationships. Women are often frustrated by their partner's single-minded focus on solving the problem and sweeping everything else under the mat when all they want is to feel heard, understood, and loved. Men are better off being patient and listening attentively to their female partners while they describe how and why a certain situation or sequence of events has made them feel a certain way, giving them time to explain exactly how they feel. Another point I want to make clear here is that women often don't make this plain to their male partners — they will talk about how they feel and use examples, then expect their partner to read between the lines and understand what they're getting at rather than clearly stating that they simply need to be heard and understood, regardless of whether the problem is solved yet or not.

When men and women fail to speak each other's language, neither side is getting what they need. This leads to a whole host of totally unnecessary problems; confusion, the frustration that in turn leads to annoyance and anger, bitterness, resentment, and often, drama. Once bad feelings are involved and the gloves come off, situations can quickly get out of hand for no reason. All that was ever needed was a mutual understanding that men and women tend to process situations and communicate in different ways. When a couple has that understanding, it's much easier to prevent any issues from boiling over.

Another issue that biological differences in communication can lead to is differing assumptions and expectations about how an event or interaction should occur. Women and men tend to have different needs and priorities, as well as different interpretations of the same experience. This can lead to miscommunication where one person expects one thing but the other has a completely different set of assumptions, even though they've both had the same experience. Men and women tend to interpret the same things in different ways, owing to our different biological makeups. As a result of millions of years of hominid evolution, men are wired to be problem solvers. To the typical man, communication serves a couple of clear purposes. Either there's a statement that needs to be made or a problem that needs to be solved. Women, however, usually have a less limited view of communication. To them, talking isn't just a means to an end, but an end in and of itself. Women tend to want to talk about their problems because it's a way to work out how they feel and order their thoughts. They don't necessarily expect or want the person they're talking to try to fix things; they just want to get it off their chest. In fact, just talking about things can often make women feel like a burden has been lessened. Women communicate to strengthen their bond with their partner and promote intimacy and closeness. Through sharing their thoughts, they release their negative feelings. For them, communication with their partner is about having a supportive and non-judgemental arena in which they can express themselves openly.

This simple difference in the way communication tends to be perceived between the sexes can lead to a whole host of small problems and irritations in a relationship, all of which add up and can snowball into something far bigger if not rectified or kept in check. A good example of this is when a stressed out wife phones her husband and tells him that she's having a bad day at work and then becomes annoyed when later that evening he doesn't even ask her about it. To the woman, her mentioning her bad day on the phone to her husband earlier was a clue or prompt for him to ask her about it later on. She thought that by hinting about her bad day, her husband would naturally ask her about it, because he's her husband and he loves and cares about her, so he knows she'd want to open up and tell him all about it. However, in the husband's mind, things look very different. It's not that his wife mentioned she had a bad day completely passed him by, but that he has a different approach to dealing with the problems he faces and assumes that what seems to work for him will work for his

23

wife. He takes his wife's comment at face value, as a statement that she's had a bad day — not realizing that she wants to talk about it. Whereas women tend to want to talk about their problems in order to work through them, men are much more likely to simply want to forget about them and move on if there's nothing more they can do. The husband had therefore assumed that his wife would rather not relive her bad day with him by bringing it all back up and talking about it, so instead he works to distract and comfort her rather than giving her what she needs.

This tendency to distract from and try to forget about problems is a real problem for some men. It is common for them to self-medicate with alcohol and other drugs, both legal and illegal. While women are not immune to this either, it is especially common with men, who aren't used to accepting or dealing with their emotions for fear of being stigmatized and outcast or labeled as weak. Many men have no one to talk to about their difficult and often conflicting feelings, which can make their lives incredibly lonely even when they're surrounded by friends and family. Women should try to be there for their husbands and boyfriends, in order to give them an outlet for their emotions and help them to process and understand them. However, keep in mind that attempting to comfort men when they're feeling upset and hurt can easily backfire and make them withdraw even more; they'd sometimes rather forget about their problems than confront them at all. Persuasion from their partner to tackle these issues can provoke a defensive reaction in men. Until a man is ready to deal with whatever issues they're facing, questions and encouragement can do more harm than good. It's a good idea for women to remind their male partners that they're there for them whenever they want or need to talk, and then allow them to come to them in their own time when they're ready.

Men typically keep their problems to themselves and don't see the need to open up or share, whereas women are more likely to talk to other women when they have a problem they need to deal with or they need to make a decision. This is because, on the whole, men relate to other men based on the power dynamic and dominance status between them, while women tend to be more relationship oriented and look for connections and ways to relate to one another through common ground and shared experience. Women focus on building a rapport with one another by asking questions, whereas men usually prefer to give information rather than asking questions. They instead share experiences as a way of competing, which often leads to instances of one-upmanship. However, men can have a serious disagreement and even come to blows over it and then move on and forget all about it, whereas women are often more emotionally committed to a sense of being right or wrong and can hold grudges for far longer. Women build relationships in order to get things done, whereas men build relationships by working together to get things done. Making communication work in a male and female couple involves not criticizing the way the other sex communicates, but rather learning how to adapt and work together despite the natural differences we share.

When men are upset, they tend to keep their thoughts to themselves rather than confiding in anyone. This can be because they struggle to communicate their problems, as they haven't verbalized them even to themselves. They're also taught from a young age to bottle up their emotions and swallow their feelings rather than expressing themselves. They're told consistently and frequently that crying is for women that they should instead 'man up' and just deal with the problems they face alone. Expressing emotions or crying is widely seen as being a sign of weakness by a large portion of men. Women, however, have no such social restrictions on them and are far more used to expressing themselves and shedding tears without shame.

The problem-solving nature of men commonly proves frustrating and annoying to their female partners even when they do take the time to listen to what their partner is saying. They tend to be looking to problem solve naturally, without even thinking about it. Listening patiently is hard for men because they have to fight the urge to interrupt and problem solve. When they see an opportunity to give advice or help or they see what they think is a solution to the problem, they will often interrupt the conversation to offer their thoughts and try to 'fix' whatever problem their partner has. The problem with this, of course, is that more often than not their partner isn't looking to have their problem solved. In all likeliness, there isn't really a problem, and they already know what course of action they're going to take in response to something. They're not looking for a fix, they're trying to vent. They want to talk just to be heard and understood, something that is an alien concept to many men. Receiving unsolicited (and often ill-informed) advice from interrupting boyfriends and husbands is an infuriatingly common occurrence for women, often leading to anger and resentment. It's made more annoying by the fact that if they just waited to hear their partners out, men would find that they don't actually need a solution, anyway; instead, they tend to jump in at the first chance as soon as they think they might have even a fraction of a good idea to help their partners. Their intentions are well placed, but fall hopelessly far from the mark.

When you're faced with misunderstandings as a result of miscommunication in your relationship, it's a good idea to be as explicit and clear as possible going forwards in order to avoid making the same mistakes again. A great line for men who seem to always get it wrong is to ask 'Do you want my opinion, or do you want me to listen?'. This might seem blunt, but if it avoids them being unable to satisfy their partner's needs properly, it's an effective and useful tool. This bluntness is the key to cutting through any beating around the bush or treading on tiptoes that might be occurring in your relationship. Women should tell men exactly what they need to feel understood and loved. Men need explicit and clear instructions that they can stick to and work to perfect. Logical steps laid out for them in an easily understandable way will help them to learn what it is their partner needs. Leaving them to work things out for themselves through subtle hints will only make this harder and waste both people's time and energy feeling upset and frustrated at the relationship. It's unfair to expect men to work these things out when they usually lack the emotional knowledge necessary to do it;

both halves of the couple should be clear about what they want and need from each other so that the majority of misunderstandings and hurt feelings can be totally avoided.

As a result of the differences between male and female communication, some women are left feeling like their husbands or boyfriends don't care about them because they can't intuitively read them as well as they might like. They feel like their feelings have been disregarded or invalidated, and their needs go unresolved. While this is a problem, it isn't necessarily true that it's because their partners don't care about them. Men tend to be less emotionally intelligent than women. Men need prompting sometimes. They won't always pick up on things. That doesn't mean that they're not in love or committed to the relationship. In general, men want to make their partners happy. They want to be good, successful husbands and boyfriends — they just don't always understand how to do this until they're shown.

Women relying on assumptions that their hints will be recognized and understood will not only get them anywhere, but it will make things far harder for their partners. When women are annoyed by their men's ineptness at meeting their needs, the end result is their male partners feel rejected. They feel like they're the reason something went wrong like they can't properly fulfill or satisfy their women. They feel emasculated, inadequate, and hurt, all of which often manifest themselves in the form of anger. When a woman makes her man aware of her need to be heard and understood, the entire dynamic of the relationship can change, because the man has had it spelled out for him and knows what he has to do to make his woman feel loved and appreciated. There's no need for hurt, anger, or fights if both partners can clearly tell each other what they want and need. If a man can manage his response, listen and ask compassionate questions as a woman explores her thoughts, conflicts will subside quickly. In the same way, if a woman can learn to understand that her male partner isn't trying to be insensitive or hurtful, but simply needs help to meet her needs, things can be concluded in a positive and respectful manner, bringing both people closer together.

Another factor that plays into this is the way in which issues are brought up in a relationship. How you bring up issues determines the level of cooperation and understanding you'll receive from your partner. Wording, tone of voice, and context are all part of how something you say is interpreted by another person, and this effect is compounded when the things you're bringing up can provoke a defensive reaction in the person you're speaking to. If your partner feels like they're being criticized, they're going to be sensitive to what you say, even if you pick your words carefully and speak as softly and gently as possible. When people bring up issues in a negative way, however, with poorly chosen words or a hostile tone of voice, such as saying 'did you forget to ask me about my day?', the chances of them provoking a defensive reaction from their partner are much higher. It's therefore vitally important that when you raise any issues that you might have with your partner's behavior or attitude that you try to be as sensitive and careful as possible, in order to try to avoid your words having a negative connotation. If you don't, all you're doing is telling them that they're bad at being your partner and they're making you unhappy, which will likely only lead to issues spiraling out of control.

It's extremely common for men to feel like they're being tested by their wives or girlfriends to see if they pick up on hints, which is a frustrating thing for them to experience. Men tend to be relatively straightforward; they don't appreciate or have much time for mind games. They would much prefer their significant others to be clear about their meaning and intentions rather than saying something different to how they truly feel and relying on hints and assumptions to get their point across.

The fact that evolutionary biology influences how we think, how we act, and how we treat others means that our ability to have a civilized and measured perspective is constantly at battle with our nature and our primitive, biological urges and instincts. Learning how to communicate well with your partner means being able to take these evolutionary factors into account when considering any issue, problem, or circumstance where they might be at work behind the scenes, and they're active more often than they're not. For example, a lot of guys are extremely hesitant to ask for help, because their ego tells them that they need to be totally self-sufficient and able to handle everything on their own. They don't want to be looked at as inferior or less capable in some way, both by other men and by women. They're even less likely to ask for help when they're in the presence of women. Women, however, are often quick to ask for help when they're struggling with something because they don't feel anywhere near as much pressure to appear capable and independent. Women will often seek advice just for the sake of taking the chance to improve the situation at hand, regardless of whether or not it assists them in achieving their objective. When a woman approaches a man (especially in a workplace environment), the man is quite likely to automatically assume that the woman needs his help. They will also be relatively happy to help because it's an opportunity to demonstrate their capability and prowess to a woman. They might not be particularly patient, however, because they tend to view this as a favor to be potentially taken advantage of in the future, rather than seeing it as an opportunity just to help another person.

Additionally, men like to assert themselves when talking to women in order to show that they are confident and that they know what they're doing, the same reason they can be so hesitant to ask for help. They don't like being seen as weak. They can also be more likely to dismiss a woman's opinions for no other reason than the fact that they come from a woman, especially if it's on a topic they feel women shouldn't or couldn't know much about. Some men also find sustaining conversations that have long points difficult, especially when it's not something they want to be talking about in the first place. This is why when they're sent long texts, they often reply to the last couple of points mentioned, instead of the entire text.

Qick Tip: These sex-based differences in communication are trends identifiable across broad populations of people across the world and are biological in origin. This doesn't mean that they're always accurate, however. Many men are very emotionally intelligent and innately understand that women need to talk to express themselves. I've also met many women that would prefer to problem solve rather than talk about the way they feel at all. There will always be individual differences, and I address these biological differences only to highlight the broad divisions in the way men and women process and understand communication.

Secrets Of Positive Communication

Communication is a form of art, and it needs to be practiced in order to be effective. In order for communication to take place, there must be at least two parties between whom a message can be transferred: the sender and the receiver. Noise can hinder this process — both physical noise, such as other people talking or music playing in the background, and mental noise, such as thoughts and feelings in the mind of the receiver that stop the message from coming through clearly and being fully understood — which can result in the receiver getting a very different message than the sender attempted to communicate. The goal of positive communication is therefore for a message to be transmitted clearly and with as little misunderstanding as possible on the part of the audience receiving it. Communicating positively is about ensuring this goal is met and that both sides understand the intent behind the message, as well as the message itself.

Here are five secrets of positive communication that will help you to become a master communicator:

1. Express to be understood - When you're the person doing the talking, keep in mind that your goal isn't to persuade or convince anyone or to change any minds. Your goal is to be understood, first and foremost, so speak in a way that accomplishes this aim before worrying about any other purposes of your communication.

2. Seek to understand, rather than agree - When you're the receiver, you have a goal, too. Your aim should be to understand what the sender is trying to communicate, rather than seeking to agree with whatever they're saying.

3. Use the language understood by the receiver - Speak in a way that is tailored to your audience. If you're speaking to a child, you should use words that reflect their reading and comprehension level and can be thoroughly understood by them. Likewise, if you're speaking to someone who is an expert in the field you're discussing, you'd use a more specific form of language with specialized words to make your point more clearly.

4. Stay focused on your task - Whatever your role is in the process of communication at a given time, you should aim to accomplish the goals of that role as well as possible. This means staying focused and grounding yourself totally in the present moment by paying attention to what is happening. If you're the sender, then stay focused on your audience — how they're feeling and whether or not they understand what you're saying. If you doubt that they've fully understood what you mean, then repeat yourself and try to explain your point in different words. If you're the receiver, you should also be paying close attention to what the sender is saying. Reflect back to them your understanding of what they've said so that you can double check that you've gotten the true essence of the meaning they're attempting to transmit.

5. Maintain appropriate contact throughout communication - Keeping both parties focused on the act of communication means maintaining an appropriate level of personal contact that anchors them both in the act itself. This can be achieved through good eye contact, facial expressions, and affirmative body language and vocalizations from both people to indicate that they understand what each other are saying. Smiling can help a lot in this regard, as can being positive and saying 'yes'.

Quick tip: You can use these secrets of communication to make sure that you express yourself well and listen intently to your partner in order to practice positive communication within your relationship, as well as making sure you're communicating effectively with other people in your life.

Body Language

Although we've historically used spoken language to do the bulk of our communicating, a large part of the expression is actually non-verbal; in fact, our body language can say more about our true thoughts, feelings, and intentions than the words we use or the way that we speak. This is why understanding our body language can help us to better understand others and forge deeper connections with our partners. When you better understand body language, you will be more able to express yourself and avoid miscommunication, something which can be extremely costly; it can make your relationships with others or your partner worse and stop you from achieving your goals.

When we're talking to someone face to face, we actually have three voices of communication that transmit messages to our audience. These are:

1. **The words that we say**
2. **Our tone of voice**
3. **Body language: our gestures, facial expressions, and eye contact**

Although you might think that the most important part of your communication when you're talking to someone is the words that you use, that aren't the case. In reality, the context of what we're saying is heavily influenced by our body language and tone of voice, and this is where the real meaning lies. We are wired to instinctively read and understand body language, even though we rarely notice that we're doing it. What's more, if the words a person says don't

43

match their tone of voice or their body language, we disregard what they say and trust what their body is telling us. When a person is sending mixed messages with their voices of communication, people pay attention to the words said only a fraction of the time. When someone's words are at odds with their actions, our gut instinct is to go with what their body is telling us. Body language is a largely automatic process. When we pay attention to it, we can control it through conscious effort, but as soon as we forget about it, it goes back to going an automatic process. This means that often when we're trying to lie or disguise our true feelings, our body language will betray us and give the other person the distinct impression that we're holding something back.

Interestingly, body language also varies between men and women, just like other forms of communication. Men usually don't give off many facial expressions in their day to day conversations and are more likely to avoid eye contact and fold their arms in order to maintain a defensive stance when talking. They will nod to show their agreement with something that has been said. Women, on the other hand, are more likely to hold eye contact during face to face conversations. They tend to be more comfortable with physical proximity and will smile and laugh more than men, as well as using their hands to express themselves. Unlike men, women nod to show that they are listening and understand what is being communicated to them, not that they necessarily agree with it. These differences are likely to be because of the different evolutionary pressures that men and women have faced throughout history. Men are far more likely to be involved in a violent struggle with each other than women, so they tend to be less open and more naturally defensive, especially when they're speaking to other men that they don't know well. Eye contact between men is also more likely to be taken as an aggressive gesture than it is between women or between men and women.

Positive Body Language

When you're learning how to communicate positively, it's important to take the highly influential role of body language into account. Notice how if you give someone a compliment, they will be likely to extend their arm away from their body and towards you, as though they are symbolically trying to push it away. This subconscious action stems from the expectation that our society has programmed into us that we're not supposed to accept compliments readily in order to seem modest and to avoid coming across as arrogant. The person receiving the compliment therefore often uses their body language to reject it, even while they might be thanking you for it with their words.

If you want to forge better relationships with others, you need to work on reflecting better body language to them. Not only will this make them feel better about their interaction with you and feel happier in themselves as a direct result, but it will also make you feel better about yourself and your interaction with that person. This increased positivity in both people can lead to a more fulfilling and smoothly running relationship between the two of you, regardless of what capacity you know them in. When people are giving off positive body language, it's a sign that they feel happy in their own skin and are confident in themselves. This aura of positivity instinctively makes others like and trusts that person more, directly improving the relationship they share.

In order to improve your body language and communicate positively with all of your body, follow these steps:

- **Accept compliments into your chest** - Rather than pushing away with your arms when you receive a compliment, instead try to place your hand on your chest to symbolize accepting it and taking it to heart. This will both make yourself feel better and make the person you're talking to feel happier and at ease in your company.

- **Hold your head up high** - Push your chin up to just above level, so that your head is very slightly tilted back. This will serve to elevate your head and help you express a confident and engaging air.

- **Push your shoulders back** - This pushes out your chest and straightens your back, causing you to walk, stand, or sit more upright. This confident posture sends out the right message to the people you talk to.

- **Open up your body** - Avoid crossing your arms or holding your hands in front of you. Doing this forms a 'gate' that makes you seem defensive, unsure, and closed off from interaction with others. Think of it like a natural barrier that you unconsciously create when you reject the reality of the outside world. It shows that you feel weaker than and inferior to others. If you hold your hands at your sides you will seem more relaxed, open, and inviting, bringing you better relationships and more opportunities.

A strange and interesting phenomenon is that improving your own body language in this way actually makes you feel more confident and capable. The very act of having the body language of a confident and self-assured person makes it a reality. You begin to radiate whole different energy from your being, giving off better signals to the people around you. In this way, making yourself more open and approachable to others improves your relationship with them. People that are less confident and don't want to interact with other people tend to have poorer relationships than those that do. When you begin to consciously use more positive body language, you will, therefore, improve the relationships you have with the people around you.

These improvements will benefit not only the relationships you have with your friends, family, and coworkers but also the one you have with your partner. You will find that giving off the right subconscious signals to each other by using more positive body language brings the two of you closer together, and cultivates a stronger and more intimate bond. When you're giving off the wrong body language, your partner picks up on it, consciously or not. They're affected by these negative signals and feel more distant from you as a result. If you can work to improve your body language, then not only will you feel more approachable and better connected to your partner, but you will encourage them to feel more positive about you, leading to them communicating with more positive body language in turn.

Reading Other People's Body Language

As body language is a language in and of itself, getting to know how to identify and read it in others is part of learning how to communicate well. For the most part, body language is subtle and difficult to pin down. It relies greatly on intuition in order to be understood and is influenced greatly by context. culture, and the individual performing it. Each person has their own unique way of expressing themselves through their body language, although there are movements and gestures that vary less widely across the population and tend to be the same across cultures.

As reading body language is always a subjective experience, one of the best ways to read it in the people that you talk to is to take note of what signals they give off with their body and replicate them at a later time to work out what feelings you get from performing the same gestures. This allows you to obtain insight into what it is that their body language was telling you by seeing how it makes you feel when you do the same thing. For example, if you're talking to someone and you see them stroking their chin, and looking off into the distance, do the same thing when you're alone and see what kind of feeling it gives you. For many people, this particular piece of body language is a sign of them thinking hard, especially when they have a difficult choice or decision to make. You can also take note of your own body language when certain situations occur to try to work out what it is that you're thinking and feeling that makes you perform a certain gesture at a certain time. From doing this, you can gain a level of insight into another person's mind when you see them doing the same thing.

The largely involuntary and automatic nature of body language means it can often betray our thoughts and feelings, even when we'd rather keep up different appearances and keep our internal world private. For this reason, it's important to try your best not to judge people when you see them giving off signs that might offend you, such as noticing that they don't appear to be as interested in talking to you as they were just a few minutes ago. We can't help the way we feel, and people will often do their best to be polite with their words and tone even as their body screams that they're uncomfortable or would rather not be doing whatever they're doing right now. When you pick up on these signals, you'd do well to take note but avoid addressing them, as doing this will likely only lead to difficulty and awkwardness. Communicating positively isn't about judging, but about understanding people. If you're talking to a person and you can see them shifting their weight, turning their feet, and looking somewhere else, then you could reasonably deduce that they want to end the conversation because they're distracted and their thoughts lie elsewhere. You could then do your best to bring the conversation to a close quickly, or move things on to a new topic that they show more interest in.

Showing consideration by doing this provides you with a sensitive and understanding approach to communication with another person through reading their body language. Understanding people builds a rapport between the two of you and increases the strength of the connection you have with them. If you can be sensitive enough to use your powers of communication to understand others, you will strengthen the relationships you have and make them feel better about you.

Another common feature of body language that you can read with a good degree of accuracy is by watching people's eyes and seeing where they go when you ask them a question. Unless the person has a response prepared — in which case they will tend to reply without breaking eye contact — their eyes will dart away as they think of their answer before returning to your gaze to reply. If they look up and to their left, they're engaging the left hemisphere of their brain, which is associated with facts, information, logic, and memories. If, however, they look up and to the right, a person is accessing the right-hand side of their brain. This is the region of the brain associated with creativity, imagination, and thoughts about the future. If they look to one side or the other, without an upwards slant, it usually means that they're listening to what you're saying. If they look straight down, their answer is being shaped by emotion. The longer they spend looking down, the deeper the emotion and the more emotion will be attached to their answer.

Learning to read the motions of people's eyes can help us when it comes to communicating better. It will give you an idea of the kind of place their answer stems from, and what region of their brain they've had to access to get it. The eyes also lend a lot of gravity and weight to a person's response and allow you to better judge their internal cognitive processes and understand them more thoroughly.

> **Quick tip:** When you ask a question and sense you're going to get an answer steeped in emotion because the person you're talking to looks down, it can be tempting to try and rescue them by changing the subject or interrupting them to help them with what you think their response might be. However, you should be patient and wait for them to answer. This builds rapport, trust, and connection with the person, as you've given them the time to let them express themselves fully, no matter how difficult it might be. Let people feel what they're feeling rather than trying to save them, and your relationship with them will strengthen.

Making a Good First Impression

First impressions can be crucial at certain critical moments in our lives. If you're going to a job interview or meeting a prospective client, making a good impression can make all the difference in determining whether the outcome of your meeting is positive or negative. Likewise, if you're meeting your partner's parents for the first time or even going on a first date, you're going to want to make a good first impression. The secret to having a positive impact on people the first time you meet them is all about where your mental focus lies. When you meet someone, the interaction between the two of you generates a focus in each of your minds that determines how you feel about that interaction. Broadly speaking, the most important focus of each person at that time is how each individual feels about themselves, and how each feels about the other person, i.e.:

- **How you feel about yourself**

- **How you feel about the other person**

- **How they feel about themselves**

- **How they feel about you**

The interaction between the two of you will place the focus in both of your minds on one of these key areas, and will often fluctuate between them. If when you meet a person for the first time you're focusing on how you feel about yourself, you'll tend to feel self-conscious and make a poor first impression because you're anxious, self-critical, and you end up second-guessing yourself and not focusing on the conversation. This can potentially be devastating for your first impression. If your focus is instead on how the other person feels about you, you will be trying too hard to please them, and you'll come across as fake or insecure. If you're thinking about and focusing on how you feel about the other person,

58

the first impression that they are likely to receive of you is that you are critical or judgmental, which is obviously something that you want to avoid. If, however, your focus is on how the other person feels about themselves, the chances are that you'll make a good first impression. This is where you should try to keep the focus of the interaction in your mind, regardless of the context of the first meeting. When your own mind is focused on how the other person feels about themselves, you create a genuine and positive impression on them.

Example: You meet a potential new client at work and you want to make a good impression. You take them out for lunch. Now, you could either talk about yourself, in which case the focus of both you and them will be on you, or you can influence the conversation to be about them, which would switch the focus onto them instead. You can then ask probing questions in order to work out how they feel about themselves, others, and the events of their life, putting the focus exactly where you want it to be in order for them to feel great about you. To them, you're one of the nicest and most genuinely interested people they've ever met, and to you, they're a new client!

Chapter Two: Relationships At Work

The area in which the average person will spend a large amount of their life and the one which is crucial in determining their income, satisfaction, and well-being in the workplace. Most people spend about eight hours a day at work, five days a week, for the vast majority of the year. This means that if the relationships you have with the people you work with are poor, you're probably going to be miserable for a significant portion of your life. A negative state of mind at work will seep into and permeate the other parts of your life, which, if left unchecked, can end up making you into a bitter and resentful person. There are two main categories to keep in mind when it comes to managing and improving the relationships you have at work.

The Importance of Positivity in the Workplace

When it comes to maintaining good relationships through communication at work, positivity is the key. This is true of both the attitude that you as an individual bring to your work and the atmosphere of the workplace itself. As a member of your workplace, you are one of the people that generate that atmosphere, and you're partly responsible for how welcoming and supportive your workplace feels.

Having good relationships with the people you work with is a vital part of your individual success, as well as that of the company. Happiness and success are closely linked, although not in the way that a lot of people think they are. Many people think that the more successful a person is, the happier they will be, but in reality, the opposite is true; the happier someone is, the more successful they tend to be. The link between work life and happiness, however, is a tangible one. If you work in a stressful and negative environment, you're going to be stressed and negative for a large proportion of your life — this inevitably seeps into your home life and forms the outlook and mindstate that you wake up with every day.

A big part of any working environment are your co-workers, the people you interact with every day and work closely with. If your attitude to work is negative, the relationships you have with your coworkers and therefore the atmosphere of your workplace will be negative, and if the atmosphere of your workplace is negative, your attitude towards it will be negative, too. The effect of this vicious cycle of negativity is poor relationships with the people you work with, which leads to conflict and resentment and makes the workplace an even more hostile place to be. It's for this very reason that positivity in the workplace is so important. If you're positive, your workplace is likely to be a more positive place. You will feel happier and more fulfilled, and you will have better relationships with the people that you work with, as well as being more successful.

The benefits of positivity in the workplace are immeasurable and extend to employers as well as employees. It increases productivity; just look at companies like Google that know how to keep their employees happy, because they know that happy employees are productive employees, and enhanced productivity results in a better bottom line. A positive workplace will generate more profit for a company than a negative one. A positive work environment also leads to a reduction of employee turnover and better worker retention, meaning the best employees stick around and improve the workplace even further by setting a high standard and helping to generate a great atmosphere.

One of the most common reasons people give for wanting to leave jobs is a toxic workplace; it makes being at work a highly unpleasant and caustic experience. Research that has been conducted over the last couple of decades by the Journal of Occupational Health Psychology has strongly linked negative and toxic workplace environments with increased rates of depression and substance abuse. Enhancing your own mindset and attitude towards your place of work through your own positivity will help to spur the same thing on in other people, gradually influencing the atmosphere of the whole company and ensuring that the time you spend at work is better for yourself and for all of your co-workers.

If you're an employer or you're responsible for other members of staff at your place of work, positivity can be applied in two main ways to enhance the productivity of both yourself and the people around you, and as a result the company. If your team is bringing in good numbers, it will reflect well on you and improve your position within the company, bringing you and the people you work with new opportunities. It's a win-win. Here's how to put positivity into practice:

Positive Evaluation

Lots of people can relate to having a figure of authority at some point in their lives for whom nothing ever seems to be quite good enough. If this has been your experience, then you don't need me to tell you just how demoralizing and frustrating it can be to give your best and never have it be appreciated, especially when you feel like you're doing great work. When you give staff appraisals and feedback, you should always keep things as positive as possible and let your staff know that you appreciate their efforts. Always fill them in on how their actions have been beneficial for the company, and show your gratitude for their hard work as often as possible. Tell them that they're doing well and that they should be proud of themselves for their achievements.

It can be tempting when evaluating your staff to say 'You're doing brilliantly, but it could be better.' This attitude stems from a place of understanding that there is always room for improvement and from a desire to do as well as possible. The problem with doing this, though, is that it undermines the confidence of your staff in their own ability. People can always be doing better, no matter how excellent their performance is. Using the word 'but' after praising your staff and following it with the suggestion that they could do better erodes any chance for them to actually enjoy the positive feedback they've just received. Dangling the carrot of appreciation only to snatch it back and inform them that they could be doing more will have a net negative effect on the morale of your workers. Instead, allow the positivity to linger and be fully absorbed by your staff by thanking and praising them without encouraging them to work any harder, for now. Allow them the chance to bask in the brilliant warmth of the feeling of doing well by pausing and delivery positive creativity separately.

Positive Creativity

After you've made sure you're positively evaluating your staff, you can begin to encourage positive creativity in addition to praising and thanking them. Essentially, all this consists of is separating the encouragement to do better from the statement that they're doing well. Rather than saying 'but you could do better', try to instead frame any encouragement separately from the praise offered. You can always push your staff on to the next level by incentivizing them to do even better for even more reward. You need to try and phrase it as though they have the chance to move on to something even better than what they already have in order to build energy, pride, and hope. This enables them to move forward and create something even better through harnessing the energy and creativity provided by a positive workplace.

If you're an employee rather than an employer or manager, you still have every motivation to make your workplace as positive a place to be as you can through your own positive attitude. For one thing, a happier workplace will make you a happier person. When you feel calm and at peace in your place of work, you are relaxed and fulfilled rather than being stressed or anxious about your performance. Positivity, therefore, isn't just about the workplace. It carries over into every aspect of your life; your relationships, your finances, your family, and your general wellbeing will all soar as a result of being happier and more satisfied in your work.

Quick tip: Bringing a more positive attitude to work with you will also bring you new opportunities in the form of raises and promotions. Your bosses will notice your enhanced productivity and your morale-boosting effect on the team. You will draw attention to yourself as exactly the kind of person who your company wants and needs — someone with a great attitude and work ethic. Someone who gets things done. This will bring you new chances that you didn't expect. Doors open, conversations happen, and things begin to move quickly for you as a result of your initiative. You build new relationships with people that will carry you further and further on in life, giving you the opportunity to put your communication skills to the test and make the most of the new opportunities that you bring to yourself.

Communication in
the Workplace

Good communication is absolutely vital to good professional and business practice. It's essential in building the relationships that these things are based around at their core — as any successful business person will tell you, having the right connections makes all the difference, and building the right connections involves being a good communicator. It's also an essential factor in building and sustaining relationships with clients, increasing profitability and the

71

effectiveness of your team, and successfully engaging with your employees. Positive communication is about far more than just talking, too; it's about connecting with people on a fundamental and very human level.

A large component of communicating well in the workplace is about conflict management. This will be covered in detail in the next chapter, which will deal with managing conflict in relationships in all of the other areas of your life as well as the workplace.

Enhanced employee engagement is one of the most beneficial results of positive communication in the workplace. That is to say, employees feel more connected to and a greater degree of personal investment in their place of work when they have positive relationships with their coworkers and management. When employees are more engaged in the workplace, they align more closely with the company's goals and objectives and help the whole enterprise to become more efficient and more productive. They also gain a greater understanding of each other, which means skills and talents that may otherwise have gone unnoticed can be highlighted and cultivated within the work environment to get the most use out of them by using individuals in the roles that they most excel in. This results in a more talented and productive workforce.

Good communication in the workplace has a number of other benefits for both employees and their employers. It leads to a more open work culture, better suited to innovation and creative thought. It enhances team building and gives everyone a voice, leading to better employee satisfaction, higher morale, and a much more positive place of work. It allows for better growth and management, and better efficiency when it comes to the use of resources.

Improving Communication in the Workplace

Putting better communication into practice in the workplace requires focusing on a few key areas of consideration:

- **Well - defined goals and expectations -** Objectives and aims need to be clearly ratified by both management and employees. Staff should know exactly what it is that is expected of them and should have their own goals and expectations of themselves that they share with management. Any goals set should be achievable in order to boost morale; setting unrealistic goals only leads to disappointment when people are inevitably unable to deliver on them. All members of staff should be aware of the objectives of every project and the organization as a whole.

- **Clearly delivered messages -** All items of communication should be clear, easily understandable, and accessible to everyone that needs to see it. It's important to speak both plainly and politely to ensure that your message is clearly understood and won't cause any confusion or hurt anyone's feelings. You should also consider the medium through which your message will be expressed. While face-to-face conversations are usually the best way to pass on messages, sometimes other means are required, such as emails or written notes. Take the time to think about the best way to get your message across to the right people.

- **Inclusivity and involvement** - It's vital that everyone in the workplace feels heard and included. Everyone should be kept up to date. If people are left out of the loop and miss out on important news and information, they will feel excluded. Part of involving everyone in the workplace is taking the time to listen to everyone and have constantly open lines of communication so that

75

everyone has a voice. Communication is a two-way street, so feedback should always be valued and respected. Fostering an open atmosphere in the workplace leads to a greater level of mutual trust and respect amongst all of the individual members of the team, resulting in greater overall performance.

Chapter Three: Managing Conflict

An important part of becoming a good communicator and learning to better manage the relationships you have is learning how to deal with conflict. Unfortunately, conflict is a fact of life. People butt heads and have disagreements all the time, over virtually anything, and if you want to be successful at communicating positively it's vital that you learn how to manage conflict properly and appropriately so that you can take charge of tricky situations and steer them in the right direction, no matter the context that they occur in.

Managing Conflict at Work

Conflict can be particularly difficult to deal with when it occurs in the workplace. Tension and open conflict reduce productivity and efficiency and create a negative and toxic working environment. The majority of conflict and nearly all preventable conflict stems from a lack of good communication. It is therefore essential that you do your best to nip any conflict in the bud early and prevent it from arising by establishing good communication with and amongst the people you work with and with and amongst any employees that you're responsible for.

In general, conflict at work tends to boil down to a deep-running pattern of misunderstanding and miscommunication among employees that sparks up into more obvious conflict because of certain stressful circumstances or events. Many employees will tolerate less than adequate communication from certain individuals so as not to make a scene or cause any drama, meaning conflict can appear to come out of nowhere when flashpoints occur that set off a chain reaction fuelled and exacerbated by pent-up negative feelings. Communication is tricky at the best of times, but it's even harder when stressful situations occur. Maintaining a positive atmosphere that seeks to alleviate and minimize stress for everyone will prevent the likelihood of such situations occurring in the first place and will reduce the severity of them when they do. If all employees understand that there's no need or place for drama at work, they will be more likely to sit down and talk things out sensibly and patiently rather than letting their emotions get the better of them and causing a toxic atmosphere.

Most conflict comes down to misunderstandings because of miscommunication. Even when people feel like they're communicating well, it is difficult to for them to know whether or not they actually are unless they have a good understanding of the communication style of the people that they're talking to. if they're speaking to someone with a different communication pattern, both parties may end up walking away with very different ideas about what is expected of them and how to go about doing it. This can lead to issues down the line, particularly if there are serious consequences to this miscommunication and people feel like their jobs are on the line, in which case they're likely to become defensive. Acknowledging that everyone has different communication patterns and styles through group meetings and training sessions can be a great way to cultivate a greater understanding of the subtle differences in the ways people process and understand information. Doing this can also be used as a way to allow people to figure out the communication patterns of the people they work with, and to emphasize the importance of double checking that both sides fully understand something before going away to work on it.

More serious causes of conflict in workplace environments include people feeling disregarded, like their emotional needs aren't being met, and that they're being taken advantage of and manipulated. When conflict erupts around these issues, it can be more difficult and complicated to resolve, particularly if there's a significant air of tension in the aftermath. Laying good foundations of communication and having little tolerance for unfair or malignant behavior in the workplace will help to prevent this kind of conflict from occurring in the first place.

When conflict does break out, the first priority for everyone present should be to de-escalate tension and end the immediate conflict as soon as possible. Once this has been achieved, a period of acknowledgment, communication, and repair to damaged relationships is vital to resolving both the root cause and any symptoms of conflict and allowing things to return to normal. This can be achieved by management and HR stepping in to mediate and allow all parties involved speaking about and coming to a resolution on the topics that caused conflict in the first place. A key part of this process is acknowledging and embracing the fact that conflict occurred in the first place, rather than taking steps to bury or hide it.

Quick tip: Sometimes, you will find yourself at the center of conflict quite by accident. Managing conflict for yourself at work is mostly about the attitude you take towards it. You should always attempt to maintain composure and professionalism by putting the job first and making sure you follow the appropriate steps to report any negative, toxic, or unprofessional behavior as soon as possible through the appropriate channels. Don't allow yourself to be dragged down if someone is being intentionally difficult or antagonistic by responding in kind. The ability to keep a cool head and think clearly in stressful situations will set you apart and help you to advance in your own role as well as managing any conflict that you find yourself a part of in a positive manner.

Dealing With Negative People

Everybody has negative people in their lives, and everybody is negative from time to time. It's part of being human. However, some people are more negative than others, to the point where they have a consistently toxic effect on the lives of the people around them for one reason or another. The important thing to understand here is that negativity almost always stems from deep emotional pain. People that are hurting inside act out and hurt the people around them in ways that aren't necessarily typical for them. The best way to deal with negative people in your life is, therefore, to approach them with a kind, compassionate, and empathetic mindset. You should always try to treat people the way you'd like to be treated, regardless of how they treat you.

For a lot of negative people, treating others poorly is a self-defense mechanism meant to help preserve themselves in the face of what they see

83

as threats to themselves, for whatever reason. It doesn't excuse their behavior, but it does help to explain it. When people feel cornered, they act out. The most negative people are people who are in a great deal of pain that they don't know how to deal with. Most people are just doing the best they can with the information they have at hand at any one time.

Dealing with negative people in the right way is first and foremost about changing your own attitude, mindstate and opinions on them. Put yourself in a position to observe, rather than judging them, and prevent yourself from engaging in the negativity. Try to be interested in understanding people rather than focusing on how much you dislike or disapprove of their negative traits. At the end of the day, no one has the power to unpick the riddles of a person's life. Circumstances manifest themselves to us and situations unfold in such a way that we're often unable to see a better way of doing things because we're too hung up on the things causing us pain.

Instead of writing people off or judging them, we can see them as the fascinating and troubled people that they are. If you can learn to see things in this way, you'll find that you're in a very powerful position; it doesn't change you, cost you, or alter your course through life to allow people to do their thing. It simply helps you to understand them.

Taking this perspective is an incredibly helpful and empowering technique when it comes to dealing with the negative people in your life. It's a way to let yourself to be in the presence of negativity without allowing it to affect your own mood and mindstate. Try to take the position with yourself that negativity doesn't have any control over you unless you allow it to. It isn't the boss of you, and you don't become negative unless you give your negativity the room it needs to breathe. In order for your mindstate and mood to become negative, you first have to hand over your emotional life and positivity. You always have the choice of allowing any negative feelings to dissipate rather than indulging them. You get to choose and maintain your own position in life. You decide how positive or negative your outlook is and make a certain attitude your own. It's a good idea to choose one that serves you well and makes you happy. You don't have to give in to the attempts from negative people to make you buy into their negative mindset.

Quick tip: choosing to treat the negative people around you with love and kindness doesn't mean that you have to allow yourself to be walked over. Distance is necessary for any relationship, and if someone is having a negative effect on you, you owe it to yourself and your own happiness to be able and prepared to put a bit of distance between them and you. Be brave and be kind, and don't let people take you away from your resolution to be kind, loving, and to act with integrity, because those things come from inside, not fromwhat other people observe. You don't need anyone else's permission or validation to be happy within yourself.

How to Deal With Toxic Relationships

Toxic people can take many different shapes and forms in your life. You might run into a toxic person at a grocery store who snaps at you because they're having a bad day, or you might have a toxic friend, partner, sibling, or parent that you can't simply walk away from because they're a big part of your life. Toxic behavior varies widely, from simple pettiness and small minded attitudes to persistent bullying and manipulation. Handling toxic people and relationships is complicated as a result of this, so we're going to break it down into subcategories in order to more comprehensively address the toxic situations you're likely to face in your own life.

Handling Toxic Interactions

Toxic interactions are those conversations and experiences we have with people that leave us feeling significantly worse than we felt beforehand. In this way, they can be compared to having a brush with a venomous plant or animal — think about how it feels to graze your leg against stinging nettles, where there's an initial sharp jolt of pain that's followed by irritation and burning over time. The same applies to have a brush with a toxic person. Dealing with toxic interactions can be handled in a very similar way to how you'd respond to being stung.

The first stage in handling toxic interactions is actually a precautionary and pre-emptive one. You can build resilience to toxic experiences by practicing self-care such as getting enough sleep, exercising regularly, and eating a healthy and nutritious diet. Looking after yourself by doing these things will serve to bolster and fortify you mentally, meaning that you'll be less affected by having a brush with someone toxic. Their behavior will be more likely to break on you like water on a rock without crippling you or making you crumble internally because you're doing what you need to do to prevent toxic behavior from affecting you more intensely.

Immediately after being exposed to someone toxic, your first priority should be to cleanse and rinse the wound in order to dilute the poison and minimize the initial effects of having contact with someone who's toxic. A good way to approach doing this is to speak to someone else in order to get the experience off of your chest and stop it from slowly eating at you internally in isolation. Confirming with another person that the behavior you were on the receiving end of was, in fact, toxic can help you to feel less alone and less like a victim of the experience you had. You can then start to try and put things in perspective. When we've just had a horrible interaction with someone, we tend to feel overwhelmed by what's happened. It's all that we can think about, so we dwell on it and build it up in our minds until it morphs into something that it isn't in reality. It can, therefore, be very helpful to step back and see the bigger picture, to see that in the grand scheme of things, a toxic interaction doesn't really mean much at all. It's awful at the time when we can't see the forest because of the trees, but some distance and perspective helps us to see these things as they really are.

The second stage is to remove the poison in order to go back to a more healthy and positive mindset. This can take the form of self-help measures like positivity training, or more professional avenues such as therapy or counseling. The goal is to condition your mind in order to frame past negative experiences in a different way so that you're able to package them away having learned all the lessons from them that you can, and then move on with it being just another part of your past like anything else. Changing the attitude you have to the negative and toxic things that have happened to you allows you to become comfortable with having had them and able to move on without them weighing you down, something which can be an incredibly liberating experience.

Another factor in healing after you've had an interaction with someone who is toxic is evaluating the type of people you want to surround yourself with. This is especially important when the person you had a negative or toxic experience with is someone who you're close with or see a lot of. If this is the case, you might want to consider putting some distance between yourself and them or even letting them go from your life altogether if that isn't enough. Our personalities tend to be an average of the five people that we hang out with the most, which means that if we spend a lot of time with negative or toxic people we will experience an amount of their negative personality and toxic behavior rubbing off on us and becoming a part of who we are. Obviously, this isn't something that any of us want to happen, so we have to be able to defend ourselves, our happiness, wellbeing, and emotional lives from people whose presence would affect us negatively, whether intentionally or not. We have to strive to forge positive, inspiring, and uplifting relationships in our lives that enhance and enrich us in order to attain new levels of peace and wellbeing that counteract negative people and experiences.

People Who Take Advantage of You

Chances are, you've experienced what it's like to have people try to manipulate or take advantage of you. If you don't, you will eventually. It's a part of life as a social animal. A lot of people see this in a very negative and pessimistic manner. They see it as a symptom of people's selfishness and greed that we can twist people into doing what we want so that we can benefit from it. Accepting that there are people out there who will try and succeed in taking advantage of you can be a liberating feeling, though, as it means that you're in a much better position to see the warning signs when a person has their eyes on you so that you can try to prevent it from happening by putting yourself in a position to avoid it or reduce the effect it has on you.

Once someone has their claws into you and is actively taking advantage of or manipulating you, it can be very difficult to deal with. Stopping a person from taking advantage of you in the first place can be hard enough, but when they've already twisted the knife enough to begin to see rewards, they will only double down and fight back against your attempts to free yourself from their grasp. The weapons a manipulator can wield are varied, but they usually involve attempts to make you feel guilty or like you're letting them down by refusing to go out of your way to help them, as well as gaslighting you by swearing that your memory is wrong and that their version of events is correct, even if you know for a fact that it's not. An example of this is if your partner takes advantage of you by letting you cook their meals, gets annoyed and upset when you even suggest that perhaps they take a turn cooking for you both, and says that you're the reason that they're upset and that if you just made them dinner you'd stop making their life difficult, and then gaslights you by assuring you that you agreed to make them dinner tonight, although you know you didn't. Yeah. Fun stuff.

The important thing to remember here is that you don't owe anyone anything. Kind and compassionate people make the best targets for people looking to gain from other people's losses, as they can often be pushed further and faster than less empathetic individuals who will shut down attempts to take advantage of them quickly and then stand their ground. If you're being mistreated — no matter who it is that's doing it — you don't have to put up with it. It's something that you've allowed to happen, even if you haven't noticed before now that it's abusive. The world can be a harsh and unforgiving place, and some of the things that you have to do in order to take care of yourself will be things that you don't want to do, things that you're afraid to do; at the end of the day, you have to do them in order to be a happy and well-adjusted person. You have to be kind and brave, and make sure you do what has to be done to put yourself first and stop yourself being manipulated by cunning, calculating predators that would use you for their own self-interest.

For a lot of people, confronting the person or people that they're being mistreated or taken advantage of by seems worse than just putting up with them and doing what they want. Being afraid of confrontation isn't a bad thing, but it will hold you back from being truly fulfilled by your life if you let it. Being brave isn't about not being scared. It's about feeling scared and terrified and afraid to do something and then doing it anyway. Life is a game of risk and chance. You might not be listened to, you might be rejected or overridden, but it doesn't matter. You have to be prepared to stand up for yourself, to have the courage and tell yourself that you're not willing to put up with being anyone's puppet any longer.

When a relationship is unhealthy or toxic, you have to have boundaries and limits that outline what is and isn't okay for you, and what you're unwilling to put up with from other people. Ask yourself what positions you're willing to put yourself in. Setting out these boundaries and enforcing them doesn't feel like a particularly nice thing to do, but it is necessary. It certainly isn't pleasant, but neither are many of the things that we have to do in life in order to survive, blossom and thrive. The simple truth is that life is one big learning experience. It's an opportunity for growth, and growth isn't something that happens when you never leave the safety of your comfort zone. If you're comfortable, you're not growing. If you want to progress as a person, you have to allow yourself to get out of your depth from time to time in order to push your boundaries. You are in control of the relationships you have with people. You get to determine what type of relationship you have with them and how close or distant you are. You get to decide how much you're willing to give to any one person, and therefore the extent to which people are able to take advantage of you in the first place.

You have to learn to assert yourself in order to protect yourself from toxic exposure and manipulation. This doesn't mean that you have to be aggressive; you can be assertive while remaining kind and calm. Being assertive is about sending a clear message to the people around you that you're not willing to put up with their attempts at controlling you or bringing you down and indicating that you're prepared to defend yourself from them if necessary. It's okay to opt out of a conversation when it isn't working for you. It's okay to walk away from dialogue, an event, a situation, or anything that makes you uncomfortable or just isn't what is best for you at any given time. You don't owe anyone an explanation for doing what you have to do to take care of yourself. Put yourself first, because that's what you have to do in order to survive and be happy in this world.

Setting limits and boundaries can involve any number of things, and is highly dependent on the nature of the relationship that you have with someone. Most importantly, you get to decide what these limits are. They're non-negotiable. If you're not comfortable with something, then set a boundary. If your friend relies on you to bail them out of trouble financially, then tell them that you won't lend them any more money — and then stick to your word. Setting boundaries and limits are useless if you're not prepared to enforce them. If you've drawn a line in the sand and someone crosses it, you need to be ready to take action and show them that their behavior has consequences. If all you do is make empty threats that you're not willing to carry out, you will be taken advantage of as soon as the people that use you get wise to your reluctance to enforce strict boundaries. They'll test you to see how you react, then pile on whatever they can get if they smell blood.

Once you're actually setting boundaries, you'll find that you come to a 'make or break' situation in your relationship with a manipulative person. This is where you get to decide whether to renew the relationship and start again with a fresh dynamic and different expectations and rules, or leave it behind entirely and move on without that person in your life. The choice you make here will be highly dependent on the type of relationship you have with a person; it's much easier to leave a former friend behind than it is to cut ties with your parents. If you believe that the relationship is salvageable or too important to let go, then you have to be committed to making it change so that it's no longer unhealthy or toxic. You have to reinvent the relationship in order to make it work on terms that are acceptable for you. The old relationship has to be left behind in its entirety. You can't go back to the way things were, because if that wasn't working for you before it never will. If you can't have a healthy relationship with someone, it might be time to consider releasing them from your life so that you can move on and surround yourself with more positive and supportive people. Release them and have them become part of your past, rather than a part of your present or your future. It's okay to let people go. Being a part of your life is a privilege you grant to people, not their right. If it's not feasible, practical, or possible for a person to remain in your life, you have every right to let them leave.

Perhaps the most important part of managing a difficult or manipulative relationship with someone is learning how to really practice forgiveness. Whether you decide to keep such a person as a part of your life on new terms or you have to let them go, you have to be able to forgive them. That doesn't mean that you're excusing their abusive behavior or advantage-taking; you're not letting them off the hook or pardoning them for their wrongs. You're not making yourself out to be weak or opening the door for yourself to be manipulated again in the future, either. What you're doing is you're leaving the emotional baggage you've accumulated as a result of this person in the past where it belongs, rather than carrying it with you into the future. Forgiveness is about leaving the burden of their memory behind so that you can go forward in peace.

Dealing with relationships of a toxic or abusive nature is always difficult, but it can be particularly hard to handle when it's someone that you're in a romantic relationship with. Being so close with someone can sometimes blind us to their negative side and allows them to get away with things that we wouldn't otherwise tolerate from anyone else, particularly if the abuse is subtle and emotional in nature rather than physical. This makes it all the more important that you take note of any red flags and seek advice about the relationship from friends or family whenever you feel the need to. Toxic and abusive romantic relationships often involve the abuser cutting their victim off from their support network, so keep an eye out for controlling and dominant behavior like attempts to restrict who you can and can't talk to.

Handling Toxic Friends, Partners, and Family Members

Toxic people can take any role in your life. They can be your friend, your parents, and your siblings. Sometimes, we might not even realize that someone is toxic until we've gotten to know them well over a number of years, at which point they're entrenched in our lives and are difficult to remove. A hard fact of life is that the people closest to you are the people most capable of hurting you. These are the people who have the most access to you and the most power over you. The fact that you're close with them emotionally and in terms of physical proximity means that you can't just simply cut them out of your life easier at the first sign of trouble, and toxic individuals will use this to their advantage to stay close to you and fill your life with their corrosive venom.

A common feature of toxic behavior is putting others down frequently for no apparent reason, which is a characteristic that can be incredibly draining and hurtful for those on the receiving end of it. Although it might seem like these put-downs have no apparent cause or motivation, they're often the result of people feeling negative about their own lives and making themselves feel better by insulting others. Additionally, some people get a sick sense of satisfaction out of making others feel bad. When they see their words having a serious effect on other people, they feel powerful and strong. They might like to control or dominate the feelings of others in order to make themselves feel good. This kind of behavior is indicative of emotional abuse, and can sometimes be pathological in nature, meaning it stems from a mental illness or disorder.

The main thing to keep in mind when addressing toxic behavior from people close to you is that most of the time, the reason for you being put down or bullied is that the perpetrator is looking for a reaction from you that makes them feel good. Your reaction, although not your fault, of course, is what perpetuates the behavior and closes the loop, forming a vicious circle of toxicity. In order to break the cycle, you have to change the way you react to the put-downs and insults that are aimed at you. You can do this by taking an inventory of your own behavior and noticing how you react to constant and consistent criticism or putdowns. When you're hurt and annoyed, you're likely to get defensive. This reaction is exactly what a toxic person thrives on. When you react like this, you're giving them exactly what they want. If you can train yourself to disconnect your reaction from the stimuli, you can instead respond with something neutral or even completely ignore the insult. Without the response they're looking for, the perpetrator has little incentive to keep putting you down and will eventually get bored and stop.

Quick tip: A good way to deal with this kind of toxic behavior and assess whether or not it stems from a place of malignancy or simply a lack of self-awareness is to use a strategy called 'identify, verify, accept'. The first step here is to identify exactly how you feel about being exposed to the negative and toxic behavior that you're experiencing. You can then verify that this is how the person wanted you to feel by explaining to them how their behavior makes you feel and asking them if that was their intention. The response to this that you will receive can range from sudden realization and heartfeltapologies to denial, such as saying that you're just overly sensitive and it's your fault that you're upset. No matter the response you receive, the final stage is to accept it. You've let them know by confronting them that the way they're treating you has an impact on you and you're not willing to put up with it. The way you proceed is up to you but should involve an amount of reflection and assessment of the kind of relationship you want to have with that person. As I've indicated previously if they're not a positive influence on your life, you should think long and hard about the kind of distance you want to maintain from them and whether or not you want to have such a toxic and corrosive influence as part of your life.

Chapter Four: Becoming A Better Listener

When it comes to communication, there is no skill more important than the ability to listen. It's the key to all good communication. It comes more easily to some people than to others, though. A lack of good listening and communication hinders relationships significantly. They can't be positive or of any real substance or depth without it.

How to Become a Better Listener

Women tend to be natural listeners than men, and can usually practice the skill far better than their male counterparts. Like any skill, however, you can learn to become better at listening by working hard on it. With a little bit of direction and effort, you can learn how to become a better listener in order to open up new relationships with people in key areas of your life as well as improving your current ones and reforging old bonds.

Listen More Effectively

Effective listening consists of the ability to focus on what's being said. All communication is essentially a process of a sender, or speaker, encoding information to be decoded by a receiver, or listener. If a listener understands not only what a speaker is saying, but fully grasps the wider point they're trying to make, communication between the two of them has been successful. Learning to listen more effectively means actively working to improve in a few key areas in order to make sure that you decode information correctly and grasp the point the speaker is trying to make as well as you possibly can. Your job as a listener is to understand, not to agree. You simply have to try and get where they're coming from and hear them fully, one human to another, regardless of whether or not you personally agree with the content of the communication.

Mental focus is important here. You need to concentrate all of your attention on keeping up with what is being said, rather than allowing yourself to think about other things or letting your attention wander or be distracted. This can be very difficult to do at times, particularly when you're in a busy or loud environment where there's a lot of different stimuli that your mind will want to pay attention to rather than what's being said by the person that you're trying to listen to. If the conversation is important, it's always a good idea to make sure that the two of you are somewhere quiet in order for you to have the chance to properly listen to what is being said.

It's a common misconception that good listening requires total silence on the part of the listener. In fact, total silence makes it harder for both parties to communicate, as the speaker will need verbal and visual cues such as positive affirmations of understanding, eye contact, and head nods in order to confirm that what they've said has been understood. Without these things, speakers tend to start to second guess themselves and wonder if their audience is paying attention or just off somewhere else mentally. If you're making a real effort to understand, you can acknowledge what is being said by giving the speaker these indications that you understand; this process is known as reflective listening and is one of the single greatest things you can do in order to enhance your listening skills. When you practice reflective listening, you'll see the speaker light up and be reassured by your attentiveness, helping give them the courage to express themselves fully and properly as they know it will be properly heard and received. When you're properly understanding what a speaker is trying to say, your reflective listening will be met with enthusiasm and confirmation from the speaker that you're grasping their meaning. Likewise, if you're misunderstanding them, they will hesitate, reiterate their points in different words, and help you to understand them better wherever there are points of contention.

While you shouldn't stay silent, effective listening *is* about listening more than you speak. You have two ears and one mouth, and you should try to use them in roughly this ratio as much as you possibly can. If you have a point you want to make or you feel like you have the answer a person is looking for, wait for your turn to speak. Don't rush in and interrupt them; speaking isn't your role when you're listening. Your role is to understand, and there will come a time where you can make any points you might have to them all at once. You might even find that listening to them completely negates the need to make some of your points or even changes what you want to say entirely.

Listening is an extremely powerful tool. If you're ever in a meeting with a great communicator, you'll notice that they listen attentively and wait until everyone else has spoken before they take their turn to speak. This is because they understand the value of listening, of opening their ears and their mind. It allows them to make a statement only once they've heard what everyone else has to say, meaning they're working with more information than anyone else had and can construct a far more comprehensive and powerful response. Having the patience to wait until last and then speaking impressively also lend these people a great deal of importance and respect in the eyes of those around them, who will see them as the most intelligent person in the room when really they're just a very effective listener.

When we don't listen properly, we end up receiving a flawed understanding of what the speaker is trying to get across to us. This can lead to us making assumptions that don't hold water and to unnecessary and avoidable disagreements, frustration, and conflicts between listener and speaker. If we instead give people space and time to be fully understood through listening patiently and with our full attention, we can have far more efficient and effective communication. Listening properly requires your full attention — you can't listen to someone and do anything else at the same time. Giving people the time and space to be fully understood will also directly benefit you when it's your turn to speak as it will very likely be reciprocated by the person that you just listened to.

Listen More Empathetically

Becoming a better listener is also about learning to listen more empathetically. This involves making a real, tangible connection with the speaker through using empathy to vividly imagine the way they feel about whatever it is they're talking about. Learning to listen more empathetically is harder than learning how to listen more effectively. While there are some directly applicable tools and methods to doing this, it also involves having a genuine, fundamental desire to connect with and understand the person speaking. This is a skill that can't be taught. It has to come from within, from a place far deeper than that needed to access more superficial levels of caring like just trying to pay attention. It comes from having a real desire to see the beauty in every person, in having the understanding that really connecting with and understanding others is a beautiful and infinitely rewarding thing in and of itself.

Listening empathetically is about genuinely desiring to get to know someone a bit better with every conversation, every day you spend with them. It's about valuing everything they say because it's them saying it, regardless of the content of what they say. It's about embracing your role as a listener completely and coming to love your role as the canvas onto which the speaker can paint a picture, a representation of how they feel deep inside. It's about enabling others to completely express themselves by playing the role of the listener as well as you can, with total attention and focus. It helps to be realistic and understand that no one is perfect and everyone will make mistakes or be too quick to judge someone or something or be arrogant or dismissive; when you can acknowledge this, you can stomach hearing them out regardless of what they say, even if you privately disagree with what they're saying while they're saying it. Allow there to be internal disagreement. Disagreement is a good thing. Without contrast and differing points of view, no one would think for themselves and nobody would ever learn anything. Disagreement leads to enhanced understanding when there's room for communication to take place. You will have your place to give your view on things if you're patient. When you get your opportunity after hearing them out, you can give them your advice and feedback on what they've said if you think it will help them. It helps to mentally take note of the points they're making and then address them one by one in a comprehensive way.

Quick tip: Part of listening empathetically is understanding that miscommunication will happen on both your and the speaker's parts; it's just a natural part of the act of communication between two imperfect and fallible people. Patience and effort are therefore vitally important parts of the communication process in order to compensate for this. Take the time to listen to the people that you want to maintain a good relationship with. Make the mental space necessary to put yourself into their shoes and imagine what it is they're feeling and why. Ask them questions where you feel like you should, make them feel comfortable, and look them in the eyes. If you do all of these things, you will be well on your way to becoming a better listener.

Important Tools For Better Communication

Improving your communication is a matter of putting in a good amount of effort as well as having a grasp of the skills, techniques, and tools that facilitate positive and healthy communication. In order to know how to communicate well, you first have to have a thorough understanding of communication itself. One of the key things that you need to know in order to really understand how communication works are that all communication is relative. We communicate through interpretation; we hear something and understand it through how we relate it to other things that we already understand. For example, if you were trying to explain something new to someone, you'd compare and relate it to things you know they already understand in order to help them see what you mean. If you were trying to explain how a sport works, you might compare it to another, similar sport that the person is already familiar with in order to help them shape the concept that you're trying to communicate in their mind. As a result of this interpretation, no message is ever received and decoded without an element of bias. We fill in the gaps in our knowledge by working off of things that we're already familiar with. This means that the message we think we receive is never the objective reality, but rather our own individual take on it. The relative nature of communication means that we always pass things through the filter of our own interpretation in order to understand them. In this way, communication is an active and participatory process. The speaker generates meaning in the mind of the listener, but the listener can only have meaning generated based on what they already understand.

Another key factor that you should understand about communication is that speech is a part of the thought. Sometimes, we need to speak in order to tell ourselves what we think. This means that when we ask people questions that they've never thought about before, they might speak before they've thought about what to say, simply because the thought is only now just occurring to them for the first time. Take this into account when you're talking to people, and do your best to be as non-judgmental and impartial as you possibly can, both internally and externally.

In 1981, Friedemann Schulz von Thun outlined the four-sides model of communication. It proposed that every message has one or more of four facets:

1. **Fact: What I inform about (data, facts, statements, statistics)**

2. **Self-revealing: What I reveal about myself (information about the sender)**

3. **Relationship: What I think about you (information about how we get along)**

4. **Appeal: What I want to make you do (an attempt to influence the receiver)**

There is always a differing amount of emphasis on each facet from message to message, and this emphasis can be intended and perceived differently by the sender and receiver. Some messages might not have all of these facets, but all messages will have at least one of them. Additionally, facets are often implied or inferred rather than being directly stated.

For example, a child might tell their parents that their cup of juice is empty. Now, this is a fact, but it could also contain elements of the other facets. The context of a child telling their parent that their cup is empty could lead the parent to infer that their child wants their parent to fill their cup up with more juice, which would make it an appeal, although implied rather than explicitly stated. This particular message may also contain elements of the second and third facets, as it shows that the child is unable to unwilling to fill the cup up themselves, which reveals how they feel about themselves, and also indicates that they see their parents as filling this role for them.

In order to make communication more effective as either a sender or receiver of information, you can think about how a message relates to each of these facets in order to consider what the true purpose of it might be, and how we might misinterpret what another person is saying because the message doesn't always correlate closely with their intention. Another factor of this model to consider is that individual people tend to have one of four different 'types' of ears that they have trained more than the others. These different types of ears are factual, relationship, self-revelation, and appeal. Most people tend to favor one over the others, meaning that they process the messages they receive according to one of these four types of interpretation. The underlying emphasis from the sender on each of the four different facets of their message, in addition to the particular ear of the receiver, means that a great deal of meaning can effectively be lost in translation. The way in which we interpret things can, therefore, cause conflict and issues where none would have occurred if we could simply clearly see the true intention and meaning of other people. In order to communicate healthily and effectively, we need to be aware of these four facets of messages from the sender, as well as the four ears of the receiver in order to take into account how our individual differences as people can influence how we interpret a particular message. If you ever feel questioned, criticized, or insulted, consider how these factors might be influencing yourself and the person you're talking to. You might both simply be interpreting the same message in two different ways, without considering how the other person will interpret it.

Some tips for communicating better include:

- **Speak face to face** - If possible, you should always try to say what needs to be said in person, rather than writing it down in a letter, text, or email or talking over the phone. Communication is a highly personal and complex experience. There's a lot of information that can't be transferred through words alone but relies on tone and body language. If you've ever tried to be sarcastic and found that it translates poorly over text, you'll know what I mean here.

- **Find (and make) the right time** - If something is worth saying, then it's worth taking the time to say properly. Good communication isn't rushed or hurried. It takes space and time to properly express and receive a message with a minimum of misunderstanding. If you fail to allocate the appropriate time to properly communicate with the people you need to communicate well and maintain some kind of relationship with, both the messages themselves and the relationship will suffer.

- **Use technology efficiently and effectively** - Technology can be extremely useful but should be used to augment and enhance face to face communication rather than replace it completely. You can use texts and emails up to a certain point in order to arrange things and transfer data that are more easily transferred electronically than verbally but don't fall into the trap of thinking that these forms of communication are a good replacement for speaking face to face.

- **Ask for clarity if you need it** - A great deal of misunderstanding stems from people walking away from an interaction without a clear grasp of what the other person was trying to say. They might feel awkward about asking the other person to explain themselves again after they've already made the effort to do so, or may worry that the other person will be annoyed or think that they weren't paying attention. Regardless of the reason why the communication wasn't effective, the very worst thing you can do is to walk away with the wrong idea or an incomplete understanding of the message. It is always better to ask for clarity if you're uncertain; you shouldn't be ashamed at not picking up on what was being said. Communication can be incredibly difficult, and everyone experiences unsuccessful conversations from time to time. If the other person does get irritated or annoyed by your lack of understanding, remind yourself that the way they feel is up to them and that no one is perfect. Everyone makes mistakes or loses focus or fails to grasp what is being said from time to time.

- **Respect and try to understand cultural differences** - The way that we speak and the way in which we listen and understand things is shaped by the culture that we're raised in. Differences between cultures can often lead to differing interpretations of the same message, which of course can easily result in misunderstanding. Whenever you're speaking to someone with a different cultural outlook to yourself, make sure that you take the differences in culture between the two of you into account. Try to understand what they are and accommodate for them as well as you can by repeating your explanation of things in different ways and checking that they understand, as well as asking for clarification from them when you're listening.

- **Avoid communication if you're hungry, angry, stressed, or tired** - Communication is best performed when both parties feel mentally and emotionally calm and balanced. This state of mind provides a natural threshold of patience, capacity for understanding, and good-will that make communication a more pleasant, easy, and well-flowing experience. If you're hungry, tired, stressed, or angry, however, this threshold is stretched thin. It's extremely difficult to be patient and understanding when you're in a bad mood and suffering from one or more of these agitated states. Communication at such times is rarely effective and often leads to problems, so try to avoid having important conversations when you're in this state as far as you possibly can. Instead, take the time to cool off and recuperate and approach things once more when you feel like you're more up to it.

- **Tell the truth** - If you don't do your best to stick to the truth when you're talking, it can and will eventually come back to bite you. When you lie or otherwise conceal the truth from others, you only make it more difficult for yourself in the long run. People will find holes in your stories and pull them apart, leaving you in a very awkward and difficult position. Lying often involves having to lie again and again to maintain the lie, which can very quickly spiral out of control and result in you having to sustain very elaborate stories and keep track of what lies you've told in order to avoid slipping up. Not only is this an incredibly stressful way and unnecessary way to live, but it hinders effective communication, will put a strain on the relationships that you have with people and will push the people you care about away from you over time. A person is only as good as their word, and when you lose someone's confidence you lose their respect.

- **Don't bottle up how you feel** - If you sit on how you feel and conceal it from people, it won't go away. The pressure will build up and poison your mind, manifesting itself as side effects such as irritability and a lack of patience. There's only so long you can keep a lid on the way you feel, too. It will all come spilling out eventually when something happens that means you just can't contain it any longer — and this will rarely be in a situation of your choosing. It's far better to vent your feelings to the people close to you before they have a chance to build up and bring you down internally.

- **Strive to avoid complaining** - Everyone needs to vent their feelings from time to time, but there's a time, place, and context for this. If you're constantly complaining (especially to the wrong person or in the wrong context) you will come across as negative, draining and a burden. Our problems often feel overwhelming, and talking about them helps to make us feel better, but doing this excessively and in an environment not well suited to it can cause other people to not want to be around us. Everyone has problems, and everyone should be able to talk about them to get them off of their chest. If you're always complaining about yours and putting your own issues above other people's however, the next effect you have on interactions with people will be negative and others will begin to pull away from you.

- **Try and maintain a positive attitude** - Above all else, a positive attitude will take you a very long way in communication and in life. Communicating with people can be a very difficult and tiring endeavor, so approaching it with the right frame of mind is essential in order to have the patience and perseverance to see it through to the end. You have to accept that it will be difficult at times and that sometimes you won't want to do it. At the end of the day, however, it's a part of being human, and without it, you wouldn't be able to appreciate life in the same way. Embrace it completely, accept the positives and negatives, and allow yourself to take on the challenge every time.

Additional Communication Tools

We've collected a few useful tools that can help you when you're bumping heads with someone and hitting roadblocks in your communication.

- **Hold an object to speak** - This is a standard tool in a group talking therapy and for good reason; it's extremely effective. It's a relatively simple premise — in order to speak, you have to be holding onto a certain object which is passed back and forth between each participant of the conversation. This helps give people the time and space to speak their minds and gather their thoughts without being interrupted.

- **Writing certain things down in order to order thoughts or express them better** - If you or someone else is struggling to find the right words to express themselves properly, try writing down your thoughts in order to better compose yourself and think more clearly. This can be especially helpful when you're having difficult conversations where there are a lot of complex, strong emotions that have to be worked through.

- **Take time out when arguing to cool off** - If you're involved in an argument, it's always a good idea to take the time to cool off rather than plowing ahead with a conversation when voices are raised and tempers fraying. Letting yourself calm down will allow you to approach the conversation in a more even and balanced state of mind.

Communicating Through Conflict and Difficult Emotions

Communication can be difficult at the best of times, but when there is conflict and difficult emotions involved, it can be virtually impossible. You only have to cast your eye back across human history or have a look at the horrible wars and struggles across the globe today to witness the sheer destruction and terror that can occur when communication breaks down and people become resolved to use violence and force to protect their own ideas, will, and dominance on others. In order to learn about how to communicate through conflict and strong emotions, we first need to look at the background of these two things and how they combine to form such powerful complexes.

The most conflict ultimately stems from difficult emotions that are built into our very nature. Although we often like to think of ourselves as more highly evolved than and superior to the other forms of life that we share our world with because of our ability to think, talk, and use the tools to construct things, the truth is that at heart we're every bit as primitive, basic, controlled by our instincts, and driven by our feelings as every other animal on this earth. The illusions our societies and cultures create act as a mental shield, causing us to think that we're beyond being driven by such primal desires. The truth, however, is that we are genetically coded to follow our emotions and primitive urges, and there's absolutely nothing we can do about it other than an attempt to manage it and keep it in check. Although the vast majority of people think the opposite, we are not the logical, rational, reasoning creatures that we like to pretend we are. We can be all of these things to a point, but it is artificial. At heart, we are ruled by our feelings rather than thoughts. Overriding these feelings and stopping them from corrupting and clouding our view of things is next to impossible — even the most dedicated Buddhist monk will tell you that.

We are prone by our very nature to logical fallacies and multiple types of biased thinking. There's a good reason for this nature; it has kept us alive throughout millions of years of evolution. Self-interest is wired into our DNA. We each have a primal part of the brain, close to the brain stem itself, that is responsible for some of our most basic and powerful emotions such as fear and anger. These are the emotions that have helped to keep our ancestors alive since the early days of complex life forms when they were very different from the modern human form we take today. This primal part of our brain isn't able to access higher cognitive functions like thinking and reasoning; these take place in the frontal lobe. The primal, reptilian part of our brain deals in emotions and feelings, and it's far stronger than our higher functions, meaning our feelings and emotions can easily overwhelm and overrule our ability to reason and use logic. This cognitive bias has evolved to maintain our own interests, regardless of how they affect others. As social animals, being part of a group is essential to our survival. Alone, we starve and die. Together with others, however, we can specialize and distribute labor, to the benefit of everyone. Our evolution has shaped us to reflect this priority. We are naturally prone to tribalism and an 'in versus out' group mentality, something that's also known as 'them and us' — if someone isn't part of your group and on your side, they're an enemy.

Other examples of the cognitive bias and logical fallacies that we're prone to are numerous. We're more likely to believe whatever the people around us believe, both in terms of our family and friends or peers and our wider society, cultures, and sub-cultures as a whole. This comes from our tribal instincts; if everyone is doing it, it means it's safe. If it's safe, it's not a threat, so it's right. Something unknown and alien to the people around us that we identify, however, is a threat. We're also more likely to believe something if we've been exposed to it before, regardless of how we felt about it then. For example, if someone tells us that the world is flat or that vaccines cause autism, we might brush them off as an oddball. After repeated exposure to these beliefs, however, they begin to curry more favor in our minds, as we come under the impression that many people hold these beliefs, and if lots of people believe in something, we think there must be something to it, because surely that many people can't be wrong about something?

The tendency to fall into this kind of dualistic, black and white thinking is built into our genes. It protects us, physically and emotionally, and leads to a great deal of conflict. It causes us to maintain a rigid stance once we think we're right, leaving us unable to consider other, opposing points of view. We become inflexible and unyielding, completely convinced that our viewpoint is right and that all others are wrong. In reality, however, there is no such thing as being completely right or wrong. Instead of being black and white, these things are in fact many different shades of grey. A person or viewpoint can be right about some things and wrong about others, and opposing viewpoints will have this in common. There are different levels of nuance, complexity, and subtlety built into every point of view and attitude. When we're unable to consider or entertain points of view without outright accepting or rejecting them, we've lost our ability to think critically and make arguments based on their merit and judge them individually, objectively, and impartially. We become entrenched in a particular way of thinking and totally absorbed into a belief without even realizing how narrow-minded we've become. We become unwilling or unable to negotiate or see how both sides can be right and wrong at the same time; this isn't a good state of mind for communication, which involves understanding that there is always more to learn.

Our most difficult and painful emotions are also our most powerful emotions as a result of our evolutionary biology, and for good reason. They're the ones responsible for keeping us alive, right back to the days where we had to run from lions and wolves on grassy plains, and way before. Anger and fear make up a vital part of our fight or flight response, which allows us to stand our ground and fight to the death or run away to save ourselves in dangerous situations. These difficult emotions spark and catalyze conflict when we fail to control them or process them in a healthy way. When someone says or does something that we perceive to be a threat, physically or emotionally, we become defensive. Our emotions are triggered and our response comes out of fear and anger rather than from a reasoned position. When we're in a highly charged emotional state, our choices fall away from us as our reptilian brain takes over from our frontal lobe. We see our options narrow and become increasingly polarized, making it seem like an outburst of aggression is the only choice we have in response to a threat. When we're in this highly charged state, we're like a volcano ready to blow. Our pent up energy and emotions will tend to take the easiest route out; that tends to be through an explosion, rather than through calming down, particularly if we're still in a situation that we perceive on some level to be a threat to us.

This conflict is never productive even when it's in interactions with strangers or people we don't really care about. When it's with our friends and family, however, it can be extremely hurtful. There are few feelings worse than realizing our emotions have gotten the better of us and we've snapped and hurt the people we love most in this world. In order to be able to communicate in spite of conflict stemming from our difficult emotions, we have to be able to process our emotions in a healthy way. We have to accept that they're there and that they will always influence us in order to really begin to live in harmony with them, rather than letting them control and rule us. If we can't manage our feelings and achieve emotional balance, they will manifest themselves in our behavior in ways that lead to and perpetuate conflict.

It's worth mentioning here that not everyone is even capable of seeing both sides of an argument at the same time. People suffering from forms of mental illness or personality disorders such as borderline personality disorder, or BPD, have brains that are wired in such a way that balancing and controlling emotion just isn't something they can do in the way other people can. People suffering from these conditions have to work much harder to regulate their emotional life and will have days where they just can't seem to get a grip at all.

Bad communication can both spark conflict and make the existing conflict worse. Conflict can make us less able to communicate, which can lead to vicious cycles where our lack of good communication makes the conflict even worse, which leads to even poorer communication and so on and so forth. When we're highly emotionally charged and involved in a conflict, the last thing we want to do is calm down, sit down, and talk things out in a reasonable way. It almost seems laughable at the time, like a bad joke, because all we want to do is scream and defend ourselves and dominate others and make them see that our views and our own interests are more correct and more important than theirs — because to us, they are.

How to Communicate Through Conflict and Difficult Emotions

Being able to talk and listen in the midst of conflict when the reasoning faculties of your brain are being hijacked by overwhelming emotion is difficult, but it can be done. Positive communication in this context is about trying to remain calm enough to allow your frontal lobe to remain in control of the situation and of your emotions and stopping them from getting the better of you.

Controlling your emotions can be done by focusing on your breathing and on your body, an activity known as meditation. You can both use this is as a tool when you're feeling highly emotionally charged and make it a regular and frequent part of your life. It's a brilliant way to get in touch with yourself and learn how to control your mind and feelings in a positive way. Meditation takes many forms, but one of the most popular and effective types is known as mindfulness meditation. This is a sort of complete focused concentration of your entire conscious awareness and being on your body and your immediate surroundings. It helps to calm and quiet your mind, and focus you on living in the moment, which is known as being 'mindful'.

Here's a step-by-step guide to meditation:

1. **Close your eyes and sit still somewhere comfortable. Try to keep your back straight, it will help you to focus**

2. **Allow your thoughts and feelings to come to you. Don't try to push them away**

3. **Observe your thoughts and feelings, but avoid labeling or judging them**

4. **Bring yourself back to the point of present awareness when you notice yourself becoming distracted by your thoughts**

You may also find that repeating a mantra or phrase to yourself is helpful. This can allow you to focus on the words you're saying and the particular feeling attached to them, rather than the other, more difficult emotions that you're

145

feeling. In order to really gain control of your emotions and learn to balance them, you need to work through your feelings independently and try to work out why it is that you feel the way that you do. The way you feel matters to other people; it's important to realize that this is both because they genuinely care about your mental and emotional wellbeing and the way that you feel directly impacts them through your behavior. Your feelings are worthy. Try to discuss your feelings from your own point of view with the people you feel you can be the most open with, and be solution oriented. You're aiming for emotional balance and regulation.

If you're struggling to communicate through conflict or strong and difficult emotions, you can take a break for as long as you need to allow yourself to calm down before you return to talking about it. There's absolutely no shame in this. Sometimes it's either that or lose your temper completely.

Helping Others to Communicate in Difficult Circumstances

When it comes to what you can do for others to help them to communicate when they're least able to, the most important thing you can do is be patient. You need to give people the time and space to come to terms with the way they feel in their own time and in their own way. If they feel like they're under pressure from you, they will feel even less able to communicate and will withdraw further into their emotions and hostility. Instead, you should show them that you care about them and only want to do what you can to help, and if that means giving them as much time as they need then so be it.

Do your best to keep calm and speak softly. Try not to judge them or yourself. Don't get defensive or take offense to things they might say in the heat of the moment. If you can be open and honest with yourself, it can inspire people to reflect those same principles back to you. You should try to display empathy and the ability to negotiate and consider other, differing points of view. By showing love and kindness and refraining from pushing the person too hard, you let them come to terms with their feelings in their own time. With your encouragement and support, they will come to deal with their emotions in a way that makes sense to them in time. Their emotional communication will improve, and they will develop a greater ability to perceive, facilitate, understand, and manage the way they feel.

Five Steps to Positive Criticism in Relationships

One of the most common causes of conflict within the context of a relationship is critical. No one likes feeling criticized, but being honestly told when you could improve is the driving cause for self-improvement. It's difficult to be impartial or objective about yourself, so we need people to point out when we could do better.

If your partner and you are experiencing consistent conflict in your relationship, it might be because your criticism makes them feel under attack and causes them to get defensive. You can avoid this by following these five steps to positive criticism:

1. **Calm yourself before bringing up a complaint** - When you notice something your partner has done that you believe to be wrong, it's easy to feel annoyed or even angry. This can translate badly and cause resentment and hostility. Take a few minutes to calm yourself down and get yourself into a mindstate conducive to discussing things. Think about what you want to say, and try to think of a nice memory you have with them before you bring up what you want to say.

2. **Use 'I' statements** - This can help you to express yourself by talking about things from your point of view, which might help your partner to feel less like they're being attacked

149

by you. Talk about how things make you feel or how they seem to you, rather than speaking about them as though they were objective truth. This can help your partner to put themselves in your shoes as well as being less likely to provoke a defensive reaction.

3. **Be specific** - Bring up any issues as and when they occur, and talk only about a specific incident. Avoid bringing up things from the past or making sweeping generalizations such as 'you never clean up after yourself' as doing this only makes things worse. This will keep the interaction at a low intensity. It doesn't have to be all doom and gloom, it's just two adults who love and care about each other, helping each other to meet their needs better.

4. **Talk about what you need, not what you don't** - The point of criticizing in the first place is to help your partner improve. You need to try and make your criticism

constructive and creative, rather than using it as an opportunity to pick holes in your partner. tell them how you'd prefer they did something, rather than focusing on what it is that you don't like about what they've done.

5. **Above all, be kind** - When we feel hurt, it's easy to forget the things that we love about our partner. Our vision narrows to the point where all we can focus on is what's not perfect about them, resulting in us treating them with less kindness and compassion than we'd like to and less than they deserve. Think about how you'd prefer they brought up any issues, and do it that way. Try to show them as much love and kindness as you can. Remember it's about the two of you versus the problem, not you versus them.

Chapter Five: Trust, Honesty, And Respect

After communication itself, trust, honesty, and respect are the most important factors in any relationship, but this is especially true in romantic relationships. These three things form the bedrock of the bond you share with your partner, and without any one of them, a relationship will be unhealthy, toxic, and doomed to failure.

Cultivating Trust in Your Relationship

Genuine trust has to be earned. It has to cut both ways; both partners must be able to trust each other if they're going to make their relationship work. Building trust takes time and effort. Think of it as a savings account; you make small deposits often, and over time your balance grows. It's the same thing with trust. There are a few things you can practice consistently and frequently that will help you to cultivate the trust you share with your partner bit by bit over a long period of time. All you can do is try your best, but with your encouragement and demonstration of the principles you value, your partner will be able to mirror your behavior and help to build your trust in them.

- **Do what you say** - Be a person of your word. How can you expect your partner to trust you if you're not reliable? Personal integrity is extremely important — it's a measure of your character. If your partner can't believe that you take your integrity seriously, they won't be able to trust you.

- **Be honest** - No matter what, you have to be open and honest. If you mess up, make mistakes, or can't stick to your word, then own it. Apologize, explain yourself, and always speak your mind, no matter how hard that might be.

- **Be genuine** - Don't feel like you have to be happy and smiling 24/7. Be yourself, be true to yourself, and don't let yourself feel pressured to pretend to be anyone else. If you're upset, or bored, or annoyed, then own it. Go with it, embrace it. There's nothing worse for a relationship or for yourself than pretending to be somebody you're not. If it's your relationship that's getting you down, don't try to hide it. There are issues there that need to be addressed and pretending you're fine will only kick the can further down the road.

- **Let your partner in** - Building trust is about having intimacy and closeness. It's about you and your partner knowing each other, as well as you, know yourselves. Trust isn't a feeling, but a state of mutual confidence that comes with the close bond of intimacy, of knowing each other inside and out. Letting someone else into your inner emotional life isn't always easy, but even little by little it gets better with time. Once you begin to let them in behind the walls you put up for everyone else, your relationship will truly begin to blossom and flourish.

- **Let it go** - Everybody has baggage, and few people ever really shrug it off and leave it behind. It's easier said than done, but in order to move forward and break new ground, you have to try your very best not to dwell on the past. What's done is done, and it can't be changed. What's important is the present, and that can be as beautiful as you want to make it.

- **Remember that you're both only human** - If you expect perfection from anyone, let alone your partner, you're going to be sorely disappointed. It just isn't possible. Everyone has their flaws. All that you can really ask of your partner is for them to try their best. If their best isn't good enough, that's okay. Some things just aren't

155

meant to be. Try to avoid falling into the trap of criticizing every little flaw you notice in your partner. Being strict and expecting them to live up to impossibly high standards isn't conducive to a healthy and fulfilling relationship.

- **Be prepared to give the benefit of the doubt** - Everybody makes mistakes, and your partner will do too. Cultivating genuine and lasting trust in each other is about being able to give each other the benefit of the doubt when things go wrong and feelings are hurt. Most of the time when we've made mistakes we never wanted anyone to get hurt; it just happens. It's going to happen in your relationship, too, so you have to be prepared to forgive and trust even when they've caused you to doubt them through their actions.

Building a Safe Environment

A sense of emotional and physical safety is essential to the health of any romantic relationship. If both people don't feel safe and secure with the other, their relationship is a toxic one. We need to feel secure around the people we love and spend most of our time with. We need to feel free to be ourselves and to fail and make mistakes and know that it doesn't matter because our partner has our back no matter what. Our relationships should be safe spaces, where we feel totally heard, understood, and supported.

For some people, this can be a difficult concept to understand and put into practice within the context of a relationship. It involves giving the other person the space to be themselves and be free to grow unimpeded. For people that are overly critical and obsessed with their partner being as close to ideal as possible, this isn't something they're good at doing. Their constant attempts to explain exactly what it is about their

157

partner that they don't like and what they would like to be different end up suffocating them; the other partner feels trapped, like there's nothing they can do to please the person they love, and like they will never be good enough to satisfy them.

Having this kind of atmosphere in a relationship is corrosive and toxic. Think of people like plants: they need space and the right nutrients and light to grow. If the conditions aren't right, they will wilt and wither, unable to thrive to their full potential. Relationships are about helping to build each other up, supporting one another, and allowing each other to push on and flourish in every aspect of their lives. A safe, supportive environment is necessary in order for a relationship to be anchored in solid foundations that it can go on to grow and blossom. Such an environment needs predictability and warmth, with the ability to do whatever makes you happy without feeling judged. A relationship should be a place of empathy and loving kindness, where you're free to fail and make mistakes and be less than perfect while being able to grow and learn and pick yourself back up with the loving mutual support and respect from your partner.

Building an environment like this in your relationship is a matter of looking into yourself, rather than looking at your partner's behavior, and realizing that it takes mutual work from both people in order to make the relationship a safe and secure place. A lot of people feel like their partner is to blame for most or all of the problems in their relationship, which is never the truth of the matter. They feel like they will always be unhappy unless their partner can change, without understanding that they are in control of their own happiness, their own thoughts, feelings, beliefs, and behavior.

You have to take control of yourself and your role in your relationship. You can change how you act towards and feel about your partner and yourself. You can empower yourself and learn how to become happier and more fulfilled all on your own, which can then in turn help to spur your partner on. You can't control your partner; you can't control anyone except yourself, but you can control yourself and inspire and encourage your partner that way. Each of you is responsible for yourselves and for journeying alongside and supporting and encouraging each other, but in order to participate fully in each other's journey and become the excellent partners you could be for each other you need to cooperate fully in thought and in action. You need to be aware of each other's needs and the differences between the two of you. You need to meet each other in the middle and be able to find common ground through a compromise where you can both be happy. You have to be able to take each other's needs into consideration and accommodate any differences in expressing love or communication. If your partner needs more words of praise and love and affirmation that you do, then you must be prepared to say those things more and they must be prepared to accept less than they would like, as long as you're making an effort to work on it.

Repairing Broken Trust

Trust is the lifeblood of a relationship. Once it has been lost, it can be very difficult, if not impossible, to get back. The person who has had their trust broken will find it hard to trust anyone in the same way again, but they will find it especially difficult to ever trust the person who broke it again. Broken trust is one of the most troubling and damaging things that can happen to a relationship. Before it is broken, most people see no reason to doubt their partner or their intentions. They have confidence in them, they have faith in the person they are and they believe that they'd never do anything that could put the relationship they share into jeopardy. When they find out about something that has happened that represents a big breach in trust, then, such as infidelity, it feels as though the person they trusted, the person they thought they knew, is, in fact, someone entirely different, someone who has only been pretending all along.

It's for this reason that the first step in repairing broken trust is that both partners have to acknowledge the reality of their situation. The old relationship is gone; it's dead and buried. Now that people have been hurt and bridges burned, the two of you have a choice to make. You have to decide whether you want to release the relationship and go your separate ways or try to repair things between the two of you by forging a new relationship together that learns from the mistakes you've made in the past. This second option is an incredibly hard process, and it's the reason that major breaches of trust so often represent the death knell for a relationship. Salvaging a relationship from an event as traumatic, complex, and confusing as this requires a total commitment from both parties to explore each other and themselves in depth in order to ask and answer difficult questions and understand all of the factors that have contributed to the current state of the relationship. Both sides have to completely come clean and own their mistakes. There needs to be total, unconditional honesty, emotional transparency, and a real commitment to change and healing.

Understanding, empathy, and patience are needed more than ever, here, on both sides. Both individuals need to feel like they can be completely open without being subject to acts of grievance or revenge. Of course, no one can be asked to not be upset with what they might hear from a partner that's being completely honest and open their heart, but there needs to be a mutual understanding that everything comes out into the open and is dealt with individually without fear of reprisals. I know of many couples where the admittance or discovery of unfaithfulness led to acts of revenge from hurt partners trying to even the score. If you're going to save a relationship, this cannot happen. There needs to be an atmosphere of total forgiveness and healing; a feeling that whatever happens, the worst is behind you. The old relationship is gone, and with it need to go grudges and resentment. This is an incredibly hard thing to do, but if you're going to make it work it has to be done. As difficult as it is, you can't allow yourself to dwell on what has happened. The past has to be left in the past. It can't be brought up every time there's a petty argument or the person that had their trust broken wants to pull an ace out of their boot in order to 'win' a conflict. You talk about everything you need to, you dissect and discuss everything to death in order to learn the important lessons that need to be learned, and then you box it all up, pack it away, and make a commitment to moving on and living for the present and future.

Communication becomes more vital than ever to the relationship at this point. It makes or breaks, so both people need to dig deep and commit to fighting for each other and for the bond they share. you need to communicate openly and with complete honesty; you need to bare your soul to your partner. It can be tempting to not allow yourself to trust a word that comes out of your partner's mouth — after all, they seem like a different person. They could be capable of anything; the person you thought knew and loved wouldn't have been able to do this to you. The hard truth, however, is that the vast majority of the time, a person that greatly breaks the trust in a relationship isn't a psychopath. They're just a person that made a big mistake, or a series of mistakes. Unfortunately, hurting the people that you love is part of the human condition.

Everybody makes mistakes, and our hearts and minds can sometimes become so wrapped up and absorbed by something that we lose all sight of the bigger picture, leaving us to come to our senses and realize what a huge mistake we've made only after it's all said and done.

Forgiveness is the single factor that will determine whether or not your relationship can be salvaged once the trust has been lost. In order to truly move on, there needs to be complete and mutual forgiveness of both parties of each other and themselves — not just for the breach of trust, but for all of the hurt both people have caused each other and themselves throughout the entirety of the old relationship. There needs to be a clean slate, a fresh start, a chance to put the past behind you and heal completely. It will take time, however, and there need to be certain new aspects of the relationship that have to be accepted. For example, the person who had their trust broken cannot just be expected to start trusting their partner again. That's not how it works. Once bitten, twice shy. Once the trust is gone, it needs to be built up again, and that will take a lot of time, hard work, and dedication. The partner who had their trust broken often needs complete transparency, including the power to access details of the breaker's personal life, such as their phone and social media accounts. Checking up on the activity and ongoing doubts about trusting come with the territory of having your trust broken, and they need to be embraced if the genuine trust is ever going to have a chance to come back. The victim will need certain assurances if they're going to be able to trust their partner again, and that means total transparency, even at the cost of privacy. That's a privilege of the relationship that gets given up once trust has been broken.

Determining whether or not broken trust can be repaired is largely dependent on the context of the breaking. One-off mistakes, while still awful for the victim, are more forgivable and understandable than repeated lying and a pattern of deceit. The time it takes for the person who messed up to come clean, the nature of the breaking of the trust, and the motivations and reasons for breaking it all come into play here, too. Whatever a couple decides to do at this point, healing needs to take place for both people to go on to live happy and fulfilling lives, regardless of whether that happens together or individually. Healing happens best when a person is able to talk about their feelings to others that are close to them. Being able to confide in someone that you trust and discussing the events that happened to you in the form of a story you tell are important — just make sure that you tell it honestly, and don't allow yourself to become the victim, as that will only create a negative mentality and cause you to feel resentment.

The final piece of the puzzle when it comes to repairing broken trust is learning to be honest with, trust, and respect yourself. This is often overlooked in favor of an emphasis on cultivating these values with the other person in the relationship. However, it is just as important, if not even more important, to make sure that you have an open, honest, and trusting relationship with yourself. Before you can look out and make real, tangible changes in the way you live your life, you have to first learn to look inwards and understand yourself.

Getting Your Partner to Open Up to You

Openness and intimacy are essential ingredients in a healthy and fulfilling relationship. If there is an emotional distance between your partner and you, it can be hard trying to work out how to bridge the gaps and bring the two of you closer together. This usually isn't a case of differing desires, as if the two of you didn't want to be closer, you probably wouldn't be together. More often than not, it simply comes down to a lack of understanding of what is needed to foster emotional closeness in a romantic relationship.

Opening up to another person puts you in a very vulnerable position emotionally. It's as if you're removing the armor you wear to protect yourself from the outside world or bridging the gap you use to keep everybody else at a distance. At the end of the day, no one can hurt you if you don't let them in and give them the power to break your heart. Cultivating openness in a relationship is therefore about facilitating your partner's ability to be vulnerable by being a safe and loving person and creating an atmosphere in your relationship in which they can feel safe and comfortable opening up and revealing their inner emotional being. Doing this is a matter of being a reliably positive, calming, understanding presence for your partner, and showing them that it's safe to open up to you by first doing so yourself. By putting your heart on the line like this and revealing your inner thoughts and feelings, you signal to your partner that they can do the same; you have as much to lose as they do, and you're happy to risk it all the same.

Creating this positive atmosphere and being a calming presence for your partner involves consistently respecting their opinions and feelings whenever they voice them and showing a genuine interest in getting to know them inside and out. It involves being receptive to what they have to say and being able to listen attentively without judgment or condemnation for mistakes they might have made or things they might not like about themselves. Opening yourself up emotionally can be a very hard thing for someone to do, especially if they haven't done it before or they've been badly hurt by being vulnerable in the past. Your role, then, is to accommodate this experience by supporting and encouraging your partner and focusing on learning about how they feel about themselves, while also reassuring them that they don't need to judge themselves and that you have plenty of things you're not so fond of about yourself, too. This openness and receptiveness will over time help to adjust the way your partner feels about themselves and allow them to feel more relaxed about the idea of opening up. Your influence, patience, and acts of kindness, big and small, will help to determine how safe and comfortable your partner feels with you, and therefore the extent to which they can really reveal their inner emotional being.

Quick tip: When a person is focused on how they feel about themselves, the predominant emotions they experience tend to be doubtful and questioning, and self-conscious. Part of helping them to open up to you is to share your own inner being with them in order to allow them to focus on how you feel about yourself, shifting their focus and helping them to feel more comfortable about the idea of following in your footsteps. If you feel comfortable enough to open up about yourself without fear of being judged then chances are that in time, they will be, too.

Staying in Love

Perhaps the hardest thing to accept about love is that it can never be perfect. I'm sure that all of us at one point or another in our lives have experienced that longing for perfect love, for our soulmate, who we'd lock eyes with and fall head over heels for and then live happily ever after with, without any of the difficulty or hard times that come with our experiences of love in reality. The thing is, nothing and no one is perfect. There is no such thing as a truly fairy-tale ending. There are several different stages of maturity in love that people go through, with different levels of understanding of each other and the relationship in each.

-   **Phase One: Yearning** - This stage represents the beginning of a new relationship. It's often referred to as the 'honeymoon' period and is characterized by fireworks, passion, and infatuation. It has low clarity, however; neither partner has even begun to scratch the surface of the other, and so there is a low clarity about the relationship and a lack of understanding of what being together would actually look like. Even though the relationship at this stage is completely untested and both people are essentially strangers to each other, the intensity of 'love' chemicals in the brain commonly make both individuals feel like they could be together forever.

- **Phase Two: Earning** - The second stage of a relationship kicks in once the honeymoon period comes to an end. This phase is characterized by a decrease in the number of love-generating chemicals and hormones in the brain, leading to a feeling of lowered intensity and even a frostiness or pulling away in feeling as compared to the first stage. The clarity of both partners as to the content of the relationship and of each other's character becomes much clearer as they learn about each other. The commitment of each person at this point comes into question as they come face to face with reality.

- **Phase Three: Enduring** - This is the final stage in the maturation of a relationship. At this point, the love-generating chemicals in the brain cease to become relevant, and the flame of passion burns down into a smoldering, glowing heat. At this point, the clarity of both people as to the nature of the relationship becomes crystal clear, and their

175

commitment stable, enduring, and lasting. Even once the relationship has reached this stage, the passion can be re-ignited from time to time, as though stoking the fire and adding more fuel through finding new ways to bond and explore each other and life more deeply. The flame of love might smolder, but it only goes out if you let it go out.

Being in a committed, long term relationship instead involves putting in the effort to keeping the love alive. Love is a choice and an action, rather than a feeling. it's a way of treating your partner and having a certain attitude towards the relationship you have with them. Understanding the true nature of relationships and the shifts that they naturally go through can make it easier to adjust when they happen to you. Keeping a relationship alive and lasting is about assuming a positive position on it and striving to put in the effort to make it work. You have to almost treat it as though you never stop dating, continuously striving to do nice and thoughtful things for each other just because you want to make each other happy.

Even if you feel negative about your relationship, this can be an incredibly powerful realization. Your relationship is what it is. No matter who you're with, it can always be better and it can always be worse. It's all about the way you look at things. The fact of the matter is, you're still with them, and if you take on a positive attitude the only way to go is up. It's always better to assume the position of 'my relationship is good' and then work to improve it, rather than looking for ways to drag it down, pick holes, and find flaws in it.

Lots of people fall into the trap of getting hooked on the passion and endorphins of the honeymoon stage of a new relationship and then bounce from partner to partner, falling head over heels again and again before growing bored, constantly searching for 'the one' who they won't ever feel their love slip away from after just a handful of months. This mentality just isn't realistic, and will only leave you with a lifetime of regret at missed opportunities with people who you could have made it work with and had a beautiful and fulfilling relationship if only you'd had the understanding that a perfect love just isn't possible to find.

A part of the fact that love is a choice that you make is that it's an active experience, rather than passive. You get out what you put in, and the more you feed into it and nourish it the more it will be sustained. It needs to be cared for and cultivated like you would a garden. If the right conditions aren't met or the proper care isn't provided, a relationship can end up neglected and starved. There are five areas in particular that need to be focused on in order to keep the bond between yourself and your partner fulfilling:

1. **Safety** - you have to make your partner feel safe and secure with you and in the relationship. This includes trust and openness with you.

2. **Appreciation** - You have to show your gratitude to your partner for their presence in your life, emotional support, and friendship that they provide for you, and the fact that they stick by you. It's important to validate your partner and acknowledge their feelings.

3. **Respect** - This is essentially being nice to your partner and considerate of their needs. It involves keeping their confidence, and not selling them out or betraying them in any way. It also includes a consideration of their opinions and consulting with them before making any decisions that would affect both of you.

4. **Encouragement and support** - Being a good partner to your significant other is about building them up and supporting them through thick and thin. They'll need your encouragement and your advice and help through all of the best and worst moments of their life.

5. **Dedication** - This could also be seen as effort, and is one of the most influential factors in keeping your love alive as it determines how much work you are willing to put into your relationship. Without dedication and effort from both parties, a relationship will slowly grind to a halt and end with a whimper as both people wonder why it's even worth trying and go their separate ways.

Quick tip: Every interaction that you have with your partner will either be positive or negative. It will either be one of love, energy, and attentiveness, or of apathy and disinterest and even spite. In this way, the bedrock and character of your relationship are constructed in the present, with the actions you do and the attitude you take, each and every moment. It's built out of the texts and the phone calls and the small acts of loving kindness and thoughtfulness. Youcan bring a certain inspiration, constructive creativity and positive energy to your relationship, or you can be destructive through neglect or malice, and let it crumble and erode away. Your choices are your own, and your relationship is what you make it. You can intentionally change your attitude towards your relationship to bring better energy to it, and treat your partner as the person you love and cherish. This way, you can keep your relationship alive and stop the two of you from falling out of love.

Chapter Six: Relationship Killers

In this section, we'll be looking at the things that can kill relationships off, whether it's short and sharp or long and drawn out and full of suffering.

Self-Destructive Behavior

Any relationship is about a bond between two people. When the relationship is sufficiently close, events and circumstances in the life of one half of the relationship will have an impact on the other. This is the reason why self-destructive behavior can be so instrumental in ending relationships; when one person is set on a downward spiral, the people around them will jump ship at some point in order to avoid being sucked into the whirlpool of negativity that the self-destructive person represents. Self-destructive behavior causes the destruction of relationships wherever it occurs, and it often leads to us hurting the ones we love the most.

The range of self-destructive behavior is wide and varied. In essence, it's any behavior that ends up bringing negative results to the person perpetrating it, whether or not they intend it to. It also includes those attitudes and state of mind that inevitably leads to negative and destructive consequences for people. Some of the most common and debilitating examples of self-destructive behavior include:

- **Criticism (whether intentional or not)**
- **Disrespect**
- **Laziness**
- **Having to be right**
- **Nastiness and spite**
- **Negativity**
- **Substance abuse**
- **Selfishness**
- **Assuming the worst**
- **Digging up the past**

- **Failing to take responsibility for your own actions / blaming others or the world for your problems**
- **Being obsessed with punishment**
- **Grudges and resentment**
- **Arrogance**
- **Digging up the past**
- **Always thinking the grass is greener somewhere else**
- **Compulsive Lying**

Self-destructive behavior is less about individual behaviors than it is about the attitude a person has towards themselves and the people around them. When a person is self-destructive, they tend to reflect several or more of these attributes in a pattern of negativity and toxicity that has real consequences for their own lives and for the people they know and have relationships with. The net effect of being a person who is overly critical, selfish, lazy, arrogant, and always has to be right is that nobody wants to know them because they're obnoxious and bring everybody else down. The same goes for people who are always negative and assume the worst about everyone and everything, or people who hold grudges and are obsessed with getting their own back. The effect is the same; they drive everybody away from them and end up killing relationships.

When a person exemplifies these behaviors and attitudes, they're hurting themselves more than anyone else. The negativity, the toxicity, and the bitterness that radiates out of them come from a place of deep hurt but is poisoning them in exactly the same way it's poisoning all of the relationships in their life. Changing these harmful behaviors involves a person changing their mind-state and attitude. This piece of advice is commonly offered and even more commonly brushed off as nonsense, because surely if becoming a happier and more pleasant person was as simple as thinking positively then it would be easy to do, right? Wrong. It's simple, but that doesn't mean it's easy. Changing a sequence of self-destructive behaviors means a person totally overhauling their personality and the type of energy that they bring to themselves and the circumstances of their life in favor of a different way of seeing themselves and the world around them.

This can be a difficult enough task even with therapy and counseling, but it can be done by a person all by themselves. All that is required is a desire to change for the better, to become a better, more positive person. Once this desire is alight in a person's heart, they will be capable of pulling themselves out of the negative, bitter slump they're in, eventually allowing them to see life with a totally new perspective. To do this, such a person must first do some soul searching. They have to look in the mirror and ask themselves what they want to do with the opportunity they've been given in the form of life. What do they want their legacy to be, for themselves and for the people they know? Do they want to spend their days bitter at the world and being a toxic influence on the people they meet, or do they want to enjoy their lives and focus on being a positive and pleasant person, who creates value for other people and makes their lives and the world that little bit better of an experience?

Once this desire is present in a person, they can go on to make great strides of improvement, first to the way they view themselves and then to the way they view the other people in their life. What's needed here is an appreciation for the good things in life, a sense of gratitude for the beautiful experiences we can have and the incredible people we can meet. It requires a thirst for seeing the good there is in the world, as well as the bad, and making a conscious decision to focus their attention and energy on the positive rather than the negative. From there, negative and self-destructive attributes can be replaced with positive and constructive ones. Selfishness can be replaced with selflessness, with acting in order to help and assist others rather than in worrying about themselves. Arrogance can be replaced with humility, with the knowledge that no one is flawless and that everyone makes mistakes. Resentment can be replaced with forgiveness, with moving on to live and let live. The negative things we hold on to bring us down far more than anyone else - which is precisely why they're so self-destructive.

A big part of what makes positive change so hard, especially after you've lived with a negative and bitter mindset for so long, is that changing means having to admit to yourself and by proxy the wider world that you were wrong for so long; that your negativity and bitterness were misplaced, and that ultimately, it was your choice to live that way, rather than it being a burden you're forced to carry as a result of the events of your life and the nature of the world. Taking responsibility for all of this is an incredibly difficult and painful thing to do, and is often the reason why some people come close to making a positive change in their lives, only to dig their heels in harder and double down in their misery at the last hurdle. Confronting the reality of our lives being directed far more by the way we react to events than it is about the events that happen to us is horrible, but it's necessary in order to begin to really start living well. We're often blind to things until they're revealed to us in such a way that the penny finally drops and everything makes sense. Sometimes we need to experience things directly in order to truly understand them, and until then, we can only do the best we can with what we have at any one time, even if those things aren't for the best for us or anyone else; we often think that we have no choice but to do them.

Codependency

Co-dependency is an interesting and complex concept that gives us a fascinating glimpse into human psychology. It's a bit like quicksand; once you're in, you're stuck, and the harder you fight to free yourself the deeper you get sucked in. It's a behavioral condition in relationships where one person enables another's mental illness, addiction, immaturity, or irresponsibility. It can happen in any kind of relationship dynamic, commonly manifesting itself as a person's total reliance on romantic partners, siblings, parents, friends, and co-workers. It's also sometimes known as 'relationship addiction' because people with codependency tend to feel a great need to form one-sided, emotionally abusive, and shallow relationships with people that they can then manipulate to provide for their needs. A codependent person will go to great lengths to ensnare and trap people that they can lean on heavily in order to sustain their mental or behavioral issues while having someone to take care of them and make sure that their needs are met.

It's commonly seen in cases of severe drug addiction, such as alcoholism, although it also often crops up in people with mental and chronic physical illness. It's a total reliance on someone else, with the codependent person refusing to do anything to look after themselves or stand on their own two feet, independently. People with codependency have to find a person that will look after them, a process known as 'enabling'. This enabling sustains the codependent person's negative behavior and allows them to continue in their lifestyle. People drawn to this enabling role tend to be close friends and family of the codependent family, and are usually people that feel an amount of satisfaction by being the hero and savior of a person in need. By 'rescuing' the codependent person in the form of providing resources and support, enablers may feel that they're doing the right thing regardless of how it affects their own life. The truth, however, is that all they're doing is allowing an ill person to persist in their illness without getting the appropriate help and learning how to become independent.

Not all enablers are willing participants in the codependent relationship, however. Codependent people are good manipulators and can go to extreme lengths in order to guilt-trip and otherwise persuade people into looking after them and becoming their enabler. They wield emotionally abusive tactics like gaslighting in order to tighten their grip on the person they're trying to get to enable their behavior, which can over time cause that person to really believe that the codependent person simply cannot manage without them. Codependency is a learned behavior, often being passed down through dysfunctional families where younger members of the family observe how older members ensure that their needs are met in order to sustain their addictions or negative behavior and repeat the pattern themselves.

Breaking codependent habits and becoming more independent isn't something that a person with this condition can do while they're being enabled. The cycle needs to be broken the enabler or enablers in their life refraining from rescuing them. It's only by forcing the codependent person to have to take care of themselves that the negative or addictive behavior can be stopped. This can be difficult, however, as they often make a compelling argument in order to persuade people to continue to take care of them. Their enablers soon become trapped, with the grip of the codependent person tightening and making it harder to escape. Relationships with codependent people are always dysfunctional due to the nature of their condition; they seep others as means to an end, rather than having a healthy outlook on the people they know. This makes maintaining any kind of relationship with codependent people incredibly difficult, resulting in bridges being burned and relationships being killed off over the years.

Control Freaks

People that feel an excessive need to be in control tend to drive away those closest to them because of their rigid inability to tolerate uncertainty. The very nature of life is uncertain; you can't control anything in life apart from the way you react to things that happen to you — your own attitude and behavior. This means that control freaks are fighting a losing battle, and the side effects of this manifest themselves as toxic behavior as they desperately try to order and control all of the things in their life.

There's a good reason why some people seek to exercise control over the circumstances of their life and the people they know. In a sense, control is freedom; it's the freedom to choose what happens. We want control over our lives in order to choose what happens to us and direct ourselves to a certain place where we think we'll be happy. The problem is that other people's freedom tends to impinge on our own, and this is where control battles come into play. Control freaks can only control their lives to the extent that they can control the people within it, and so they're constantly trying to shape and mold others into being what *they* want them to be, rather than respecting the right of individuals to be independent and make their own choices.

Controlling relationships can happen anywhere, but they most commonly crop up in dynamics where the controlling person naturally has a great deal of control over another, such as parents or romantic partners, and it is, therefore, less of a stretch to control more and more of a person's life as they're already closely linked. Because people tend to be naturally independent, the behavior of control freaks only makes the people in their life pull further away from them in an attempt to avoid being caught up in the way the control freak wants everything in their life to be ordered. This means that controlling behavior often only ends one way — with breakups, friends pulling away, and children getting out of the family home as soon as they can in order to live their own lives on their own terms.

Becoming a less controlling person is about coming to not only tolerate but appreciate the uncertainty and chaos that are the natural state of life. Rather than seeking to have everything run according to their expectations, the controlling person must come to understand that all they can really control is the way they react to life and that the beauty and enjoyment in life come from going with the flow rather than trying to swim against the current. People have the right to self-determination, and they will do what they will. There's no way to prevent people from hurting you, either. If someone is going to hurt or betray you, then it's going to happen, and there's nothing that can be done to prevent or control it.

Insecurity

Everyone feels insecure from time to time, but when it becomes a defining part of our everyday life, insecurity can become very troublesome for our own self-esteem and the relationships we have with other people in our lives, with whom we're constantly second-guessing the opinions and thoughts of and seeking reassurance and validation from. Although insecurity can affect all kinds of relationships, it is at its most destructive in romantic ones, where so much of ourselves and our own identity is placed in the bond we have with another person and questions surrounding what they truly think about us, whether or not we're good enough for them, if they think we're good enough, if we're smart enough or good looking enough and whether they accept us or not all come bubbling to the surface in spates of anxiety and worry. This need for other people's approval undermines our confidence and trust in ourselves, pulling us further and further away from feeling happy in

197

our own bodies and minds and towards needing constant validation and acceptance from other people in order to maintain a feeling of self-worth.

This problem has been exacerbated significantly in the age of social media, where we can upload pictures of ourselves in order to receive quantifiable feedback about how loved or admired or appreciated we are from the people we know. We all want to feel secure and confident, and often we don't. It's the nature of life. When this issue gets out of hand, though, it can turn us into a black hole, sucking in reassurance and validation of others at ever increasing rates, trying to fill a void inside of us that can never be filled by the acceptance and love of anyone other than ourselves. This can be especially problematic when it comes to our partners and significant others, as the insecurity that causes us to fall in upon ourselves can take hold of them and bring them down with us. Our unquenchable thirst for their approval and reassurance can lead to them feeling drained and as though they're not enough for us, which in a sense, they aren't. No one can ever be enough for an insecure person. No amount of outside approval and validation will ever fill the void they feel deep inside. Only their own love and approval and acceptance will be able to heal this wound.

Overcoming insecurity, first of all, requires an understanding of why we feel insecure. It's okay to be insecure, but we have to figure out where it's coming from in order to fix it. The self-consciousness and doubt we feel towards ourselves when we're insecure ultimately stems from our focus on how other people feel about us and how we feel about ourselves. We're totally absorbed by and tied up with ourselves; with the way we're perceived by others and by ourselves. This causes us a great deal of anxiety because we're constantly worrying about how we appear to other people and what they think about us. In reality, it doesn't matter what anyone thinks about you. All that is important is how you feel about yourself.

Although it might seem counterintuitive, becoming more comfortable with ourselves requires getting out of our own way and realizing that how we feel about ourselves or how other people perceive us is irrelevant. Instead, we can focus on how others perceive themselves in order to distract us from constantly second-guessing ourselves and worrying about how we appear. We can use 'metacognition' or think about thinking, to learn about how our minds process our relationship with ourselves. We can then notice that we have a much higher level of choice and control over how we feel about ourselves than we might have previously thought. We become more confident in ourselves and comfortable in our own skin when we realize that we are good enough, that we have always been good enough because we are who we are and that's okay, no matter who we are.

Quick tip: We have to embrace all of the things that make us unique, both good and bad. We have to accept our flaws and realize that everybody else is just as flawed and just as capable of being a villain as we are. It's only when we come to the understanding that everyone feels insecure and doubts themselves sometimes that we realize we have to love and accept ourselves first and foremost. We can express gratitude for our lives and the opportunity we have by focusing on how others feel about themselves, rather than on how they feel about us or how we feel about ourselves.

Fixing a Broken Relationship

Romantic relationships are incredibly confusing and complicated. Navigating them is one of the hardest things we have to do in our lives. In order to heal rifts and fix a relationship, the first step is to find out what exactly it is that's broken. Just like taking a car to the mechanic or going to the doctor, you have to make a diagnosis before you can begin taking steps to address and solve the problem. This is where the majority of couples get in trouble when it comes to trying to fix issues in their relationship — they can't figure out where the real problem lies because they get bogged down on blaming each other and worrying about who is right or wrong. In reality, no one is right and no one is wrong. When there are issues in a relationship, the blame is always shared. Working out who is right and who is wrong isn't important; making a diagnosis is.

In order to fix a relationship, you first have to take a step back and realize that the two of you are a team. The mentality you need to have as a couple in order to overcome obstacles is that it's the two of you versus the problem. Trying to work out who's right and who's wrong and placing the blame on each other only separates you and pushes you further apart when what you really need is to make a stand together and use teamwork and mutual support to figure out the problems and tackle them as a unit. You have to set your ego aside and embrace the idea of working together in order to float rather than stepping on each other trying to grasp for air. If you take the latter approach, the relationship will drown. You are entitled to feel however you want to feel, but if you really want to make things work, you have to commit to being a team.

Communication is key. Commit to the journey of life together, to continue learning about each other and pushing the depths of your understanding deeper and further. Talk to each other, be open and honest, and give each other the time and space to really hear each other out.

If you want to make things work, then love hasn't been lost. Sometimes it just takes a different way of seeing things in order to rediscover all the incredible things that you've come to take for granted in each other. Life is short, so try not to take things too seriously. Try to lighten up, enjoy each other's company and have some fun. Be nice to each other, and remember that no matter what happens, you're in it together.

Chapter Seven: Ending Relationships

Part of being a good communicator and understanding relationships involves knowing how to bring them to a close in a positive way when it's time to call it a day. In this section, we'll be looking at how to do exactly that.

Breaking Up in the Right Way

The reality of life is that many relationships have to come to an end sooner or later. We can't all be with the first person we date forever. Communication is as essential in ending relationships as it is in maintaining them. The way in which we break up with our partners directly determines the amount of suffering and heartache that they feel. When we handle things maturely and respectfully through the good use of communication skills, we can keep the agony our partner feels at being broken up with to a minimum.

- **Make sure you're certain** - Once you play the breakup card, you can't take it back. Breaking up is now on the table, and even if you decide that you've made a mistake and you want to be together, after all, it won't come off. The first fight or disagreement will only drag everything back up again. If you're not certain about what you want to do, then wait and do nothing until you're totally sure of how you feel. You can't afford to make any rash decisions with so much at stake.

- **Once you've made up your mind, end things quickly** - When you know what you want and need to do, do it as soon as possible. You have to make a sharp break. Life is desperately short, so you have to do what's right for both of you. It's not fair on you or them to go on if you're not happy with the way things are. If you've got plans made such as a holiday booked or a birthday you've bought a present for, you'll need to be brave. Those things don't matter in the long run, and you'll feel extremely strange the whole time if you know you're just biding your time until you break up with them. There's never a perfect time to break up, so do it quickly.

- **Don't be unfair** - Clumsy lovers sometimes can't bring themselves to be the bad guy by ending a relationship that they don't want to be a part of anymore, so they do something to force their partner's hand like starting to drink a lot or cheat. Don't be unfair, and don't make things any harder or more painful than they have to be.

- **Do it in person** - You owe your partner enough to be able to break up with them face to face. Spare them the added pain and humiliation of being broken with over the phone or through text.

- **Tell them the facts, keep it specific** - You don't need to be nasty about it by bringing up every tiny flaw and minor detail you've ever disliked about them. What you do have to do is lay out the facts of why you're breaking up with them as clearly as you can, keeping it specific and sticking to the basic information. Explain how you're not right for each other, and admit the wrongs and difficulties that you bring to the relationship to help them to see that it's for the best for both of you if you go your separate ways.

- **Be brave** - You're probably going to be hated by your partner and possibly their friends and family for a while after you call it quits, so be courageous and hang in there. You're doing the right thing if you no longer want to be with them, so don't worry about justifying it to anyone other than yourself.

- **Put yourself in their shoes** - Be as emotionally mature as you can and handle things with tact. Your partner is going to be experiencing a great deal of pain and sadness. They're going to feel the sorrow of losing someone they liked and loved. We often only think about ourselves and how we're gonna take things like this, but it's important for us to put ourselves in their shoes and think about how they're going to feel and what the best way of doing things is before we pull the trigger.

- **Prepare yourself emotionally** - The longer you spend with someone, the more of your life will look strange and weird in retrospect after you break up with them. You'll find you're no longer sure how to feel about all of the memories and souvenirs you have from the relationship, but you have to keep in mind that just because things didn't work out, in the long run, doesn't make the time you spent with them wasted. Be glad that you had the opportunity to make those memories and have those experiences. Regardless of whether or not you feel relieved once you've ended things, you're going to feel horrible afterward. Relationships are a habit, so you'll feel an element of withdrawal once it's over. You'll also lose a lot of emotional support, which can be difficult to process. Take the time to prepare yourself, and hang out with your friends and family to help get you through it.

- **Be committed** - Once you've broken up, go 'no contact'. Let them and yourself heal by distancing yourself. Don't flip flop on your decision. Breaking up is hard enough, so you owe it to the person you've been with for however long to try and break the news to them in a way that is respectful without dangling the thread and giving them hope for a future between the two of you if none exists.

Staying Friends

Whether or not you can stay friends with your ex after the two of you break up depends on the context of your relationship and the manner of your breakup. If you ended things on good terms, with mutual understanding and respect, the odds are better for you to have to maintain a positive friendship with them than if it ends with hostility. Remaining friends after a breakup is difficult, however, as the relationship has been forever changed. It's very hard, if not impossible to be close friends — it's weird going from being so close and intimate to a step down from that. You might find that you begin to feel things that you don't want to feel for them. Being on friendly but more distant terms is far more pragmatic. It's highly dependent on how willing both of you are to stay in touch and to what extent you want to remain a part of each other's lives. Maybe it will work, and maybe it won't. All you can do is wait and see what happens.

If the breakup was a divorce or you have children together, things can be more complicated. You might have to remain on friendly terms for the sake of your kids, or in order to get through the divorce proceedings with the minimum amount of hassle possible. At the end of the day, you can't control hey they feel or what they want to do, so all you can do is look after yourself and enjoy a rich and full life on your own. That way, you're in a position to have that relationship with them if it turns out to be an option, but if not, it's not the end of the world. It's important to be financially independent and completely self-reliant if you have children so that you're not dependent on child support and whatever you do get is a bonus, rather than simply being what is expected.

Whatever happens, go forward with your head held high and know that no matter what, life is what you make it. Partners come and go, and although you'll miss them at first, if they're no longer with you, it's for a reason.

Final Words

Communication is one of those skills that everyone possesses but few know how to truly use. Not many people even understand the true potential that communication has to change lives and revolutionize the way you feel about yourself and others. It is the key to living in a way that is successful and fulfilling, and with this book, you've gained the knowledge and the tools to implement it properly in every area and aspect of your life. You've learned about the differences between men and women in terms of how communication is understood and processed, and how to take these differences into account when you communicate. You've learned about how to implement positive communication, how to read body language in order to properly understand the message someone is putting across, and how to make a great first impression on someone every time through the focus of your communication with them.

We've gone over how to communicate and manage relationships at work, as well as how to manage conflict, deal with difficult, negative, and toxic people, and how to know when it's time to remove these people from your life. As social animals, being able to talk to each other and interact is the primary ether through which we construct our lives. Communication makes up the basis of our societies and our individual lives, and the people we share our experiences with are the true determinators of what kind of experience we have in this world. Being able to sustain healthy and balanced relationships with the people we know is therefore essential to being a happy and well-rounded person surrounded by people that uplift and inspire us and who we encourage and support as much as we can. Relationships are mutual, shared experiences, and improving them will help to improve both your lives in a way that you never could have imagined before.

It's my hope that this book has been able to coach you through taking a more proactive and understanding approach to the most important relationships in your life. I hope it has enabled you to better understand the importance of trust, honesty, and respect in forming and maintaining relationships with the people in your life, as well as allowing you to gain a clearer view of those traits and behaviors that can bring relationships to a short, sharp end. Learning all of these things will not only help you to become a better communicator and master of relationships, but also to become a happier, more confident, and deeply fulfilled person.

This book has shown you how to incorporate a more thoughtful and measured approach to communication in every area of your life and will enable you to form and maintain lasting bonds with the great people you meet and sustain and nourish the relationships that you have with the people you love. Life is a minefield, so with this book, I've done my best to communicate the importance and gravity of practicing patience and understanding when it comes to communicating with the people in your life. Everyone is fighting their own internal battles, so having the ability to step back and be impartial in order to deliver a measured and thoughtful response puts you in the very top percentile of communicators on the planet. With the skills you've learned here, you're now ready to get out there and revolutionize the approach you take to communicating with the people you know in a more positive and beneficial way. You'll be able to tackle and handle relationships no matter the context and work out how to get yourself through sticky situations. You'll be able to change your relationship with your partner, friends, and family for the better, and more easily understand why the people in your life do and say the things they do. This ability can be incredibly useful in the weary journey through complex relationships and difficult circumstances that we all face. It will provide clarity and indicate to you the right course of action where before you would have been stumped. Embrace your life and the people in it, and remember that happiness is always best when it's shared.

Life is short, so at the end of the day, all you can do is try your best and surround yourself with good people. When this isn't possible, this book has shown you the way to manage relationships in order to bring those that have run their course to a close and allow you to move ahead towards a brighter, more positive future with the people in your life that uplift and support you, rather than with negative and toxic people who are on a downward path and are only concerned with bringing you down with them. Cut those people loose wherever you can — your life can only improve without them — and remember that you're shaped and defined by the people that you spend the most time with. Spend time with the right people, with positive and encouraging people, and let those who will make your life worse drift away.

I hope you've enjoyed reading it as much as I enjoyed writing it, and that the lessons it has taught you are as beneficial and essential to changing your life for the better as they have been for mine. Remember that your life is in your hands and the relationships you have are completely within your control. All it takes is the desire to shape your life for the better and the know-how that this book has provided you with. Be kind, be brave, and remember to be patient and understanding as much as you can. Communication is as much about really understanding the background around how people's minds work and the reasons they do what they do as it is the raw essence of getting a message across. If you can give people the time and space they need, they'll be able to tell you what they want you to know in their own time.

Good luck!